Date Due

MY 05 '95			
NO 29 99			

Children
of
Exceptional Parents

The *Journal of Children in Contemporary Society* series:

Children
of
Exceptional Parents

Edited by
Mary Frank, MS in Education

The Haworth Press
New York

Children of Exceptional Parents has also been published as *Journal of Children in Contemporary Society*, Volume 15, Number 1, Fall 1982.

The Haworth Press, Inc., 28 East 22 Street, New York, NY 10010

Library of Congress Cataloging in Publication Data
Main entry under title:

Children of exceptional parents.

(The journal of children in contemporary society; v. 15, no. 1)
Includes bibliographies.
1. Children of alcoholic parents—Addresses, essays, lectures. 2. Children of the mentally ill—Addresses, essays, lectures. 3. Children of prisoners—Addresses, essays, lectures. I. Frank, Mary, 1919-   . II. Series.
HV5132.C48 1983   362.7'044   82-25481
ISBN 0-917724-96-8

Children of Exceptional Parents

Journal of Children in Contemporary Society
Volume 15, Number 1

CONTENTS

Children
of
Exceptional Parents

Introduction

The broad range of exceptional children has been of intense concern to those in the human services for the past 25 years. Of more recent, and growing, concern to professionals as well as to those in our wider society are the children of exceptional parents. Four main areas have concerned professionals: the cause whether it be related to genetic, inherited, or environmental problems; the impact these problems have on family relationships and child rearing patterns, the intervention strategies which would prevent a second generation with similar problems, and the need to establish social agencies and organizations both at the local and national level which offer treatment and support for the various exceptionalities.

The intent of this issue is to bring together the most recent research and intervention strategies which have addressed these concerns in three areas of exceptionality. They are the alcoholic parent, the mentally ill parent, and the incarcerated parent. The first two areas were selected because they, primarily, cut across large segments of our population regardless of social-economic class, race, and sex. The latter, the incarcerated parent, was chosen because until recently professionals and society have been less committed to understanding the impact of incarceration on families and children. Through the joint efforts of many grass-roots groups, professionals, and social agencies, more national attention and support are being given to the spouse and children of offenders.

The contributors to this issue are nationally recognized in the fields of child development, social work, social science, medicine, psychology, and psychiatry. In reviewing the contents of this issue it is interesting to note both that these contributors from different disciplines have identified several commonalities which exist among the various areas of exceptionality and that some of the research disproves previously believed assumptions.

We are grateful to these contributors for their noteworthy contributions as well as appreciative to Dr. Naomi Ragins, Margaret Moore,

1

James Murphy, Ned Pfundt, Pat Malloy, and William Morse who contributed their expertise and time to the initial development of this issue.

MIF

The Offspring of Alcoholics: Outcome Predictors

Nady el-Guebaly, MD

ABSTRACT. The risk of psychosocial problems related to drinking being present among the "grown-up" children of alcoholics is reviewed. The genetic predisposition is so far the best predictor available. It may be more influential near the severe end of the illness spectrum and less so in females. It may lead to differences in symptomatology and management. The Environmental causal links are more difficult to control for in designs studying the kinds of stresses within the family that may heighten the risk for the development of alcoholism. Poverty, family disorganization, antisocial behavior and alcoholism often occur together, their etiological relationship has not yet been determined. One must not, however, forget that a significant group of alcoholics does not have an alcoholic parent. An analysis of the source of the strengths of offspring of alcoholics should be as important as that of their handicap in assessing the genetic versus environmental contributions.

Alcoholism has long been recognized as a problem that affects not only the alcoholic but his/her environment, including his/her children. These children have been referred to variously as "the forgotten children" (Cork, 1969), "the hidden tragedy" (Bosma, 1972), and "a neglected problem" (Sloboda, 1974).

Research in the field attempts to delineate areas of disadvantage

Dr. el-Guebaly is Associate Professor, University of Manitoba, and Head, Department of Psychiatry, St. Boniface General Hospital, 409 Tache Avenue, Winnipeg, Manitoba, R2H 2A6, Canada.

3

that result from having an alcoholic as a parent and new findings are often added to an already long list of problems. The range and, in many cases, the contradictions among these findings prompted us to monitor the literature that has appeared on this subject over the past 30 years (el-Guebaly & Offord, 1977 & 1979). The manner in which the samples were collected and the ages of the offspring considered, the criteria used for the diagnosis of alcoholism in the parents and of emotional disturbance in the offspring, the conclusions and their suitability for generalization and the issues raised for future consideration received particular attention. This article's goal is to review the studies, aiming at eliciting valid predictors of the risk of psychosocial problems related to drinking present among the "grown-up" children of alcoholics. (Editor's note: For specific studies grouped according to the age of offspring of alcoholics, refer to Moorehouse and Richards' article).

THE GENETIC INFLUENCE

Increasingly sophisticated designs are available to study the genetic influences of the adult behavior of offspring of alcoholics.

Study of relatives. Amark in 1951 studied first-degree relatives of 203 alcoholics seen at psychiatric clinics and reported findings compatible with a genetic contribution to the origin of psychopathy in certain groups of alcoholics. Winokur et al. (1970) focussed on alcoholism, affective disorders, and sociopathy among the sons and daughters of 259 alcoholic probands. Sons of alcoholics had an increased morbidity risk for alcoholism, while the daughters were at higher risk for affective disorders. This morbidity increased further for daughters of female alcoholics (71% versus 44% for daughters of male alcoholics). The importance of directly interviewing the relatives, rather than relying on information obtained from the alcoholic probands was stressed (Rimmer & Chambers, 1969).

Twin studies. Kaij (1960) sampled 214 probands in Sweden from "the registers of abusers of alcohol" who were members of 174 twin pairs—48 pairs were monozygotic (MZ) and 126 were dizygotic (DZ). Of the MZ probands, 54.2% had twins who were also alcoholics compared with 31.5% of the DZ probands. Another Scandinavian twin study (Partenen et al., 1966) suggested an influence of heredity on the frequency and amount of drinking but not on "problem drinking."

Sex-linked inheritance. Cruz-Coke and Varela (1966) attempted to correlate alcoholism with color blindness in their review of X-linked inheritance. A more recent study by Kaij and Dock did not support this finding (1975). They compared sons-of-sons and sons-of-daughters of male alcoholics and found a high risk for alcoholism but no substantial difference between the two groups of grandsons.

Foster design. Roe and Burks (1945) found no significant difference in adult adjustment between a group of 36 foster children of alcoholic parentage (21 males, 15 females) and 25 foster children with non-alcoholic biological parents (14 females, 11 males). In addition, no alcoholism was found in any of the children; the authors concluded that heredity did not play a determining role in the etiology of alcoholism. Goodwin et al. (1973) criticized the study by Roe and Burks for dealing with a small sample, almost half of whom were females, who are a lower risk for alcoholism in general.

Half-sibling design. Schuckit et al. (1972) used as probands those consecutive admissions to the alcohol unit of a state hospital with half-siblings. In all, 60 males and 9 females aged 22–54 were interviewed along with 90 of their relatives. The incidence of alcoholism in children with an alcoholic biological parent who had been raised by a non-alcoholic parent figure was compared with the incidence in children who did not have an alcoholic parent but were raised by an alcoholic parent figure. Similarly, children with and without alcoholic biological parents who shared their childhood homes with alcoholic probands were compared. For each comparison, the genetic factor seemed to be more closely associated with alcoholism than the environmental one.

Adoptees design. Goodwin et al. (1973) studied Danish non-family adoptees from a pool of 5,483; they found 55 males who had been separated from their biological parents within the first 6 weeks of life who had one parent with a hospital diagnosis of alcoholism. These 55 males were compared to two control groups, one of 28 subjects with parental psychiatric hospitalization for reasons other than alcoholism and another of 50 subjects with no parental psychiatric hospitalization. Subjects were matched for age, sex, and time of adoption. The adoptive parents of index and control subjects were of similar socioeconomic class and had similar rates of alcoholism and other psychiatric disorders. Examinations of the various groups were done blindly. On Goodwin's criteria, the alcoholism rate of the probands was almost 4 times that of the control group. The two groups did not differ significantly on milder forms of drinking or character disorder. The data were interpreted as favoring a "genetic predisposition" for the severe alcoholism end of the spectrum of problem drinking. Subsequently, a subgroup of the adoptees sample—adopted sons of alcoholics who had brothers (both full and half-siblings) raised by their alcoholic biological parent—along with controls, were given a blind psychiatric interview (Goodwin et al., 1974). Both adopted and non-adopted sons had high rates of alcoholism (25% and 17%, respectively) but the difference between their rates and that of the controls was not statistically significant. The two groups also had comparable frequencies of other drinking categories. Severity of the parent's alcoholism (measured by number of hospitalizations) rather than length of exposure to the alcoholic parent was positively related to alcoholism in the offspring. According to the authors, "simply living with an alcoholic parent appeared to have no relationship to the development of alcoholism."

These findings have been duplicated. In a recent publication, Cadoret et al. (1980) using adoption records in Iowa identified 167 male adoptees aged 18 years and older; of these only a final sample of 92 were able to be included as subjects. A possible sample bias, common in studies involving interviewing adoptive parents and adoptees is present yet from the available characteristics the refusers and cooperators looked similar. In this sample the environmental variables, taken alone, explained less the presence of alcoholism in adoptees than the biologic predictors taken alone and when the environmental variables were added to the biologic background variables, prediction of adoptee alcoholism did not improve. There was no evidence either that environmental variables potentiated or ameliorated the risks of adoptee alcoholism due to biologic background. Alcoholism is often contaminated with antisocial personality but alcoholism in biologic relatives specifically predicted adoptee alcoholism, regardless of presence or absence of adoptee antisocial personality.

The above set of research lends support to a genetic etiological contribution to some form of alcoholism.

THE ENVIRONMENTAL INFLUENCE

Several studies focus on the early experiences of the alcoholic's "growing up" and the rearing influences he/she was exposed to.

Parental loss. Hilgard and Newman (1963) compared a population of hospitalized schizophrenics (N = 1,561) and alcoholics (N = 929), all native-born (aged 20–49), with a group controlled for age only from a nearby town (N = 1,090). They found earlier maternal loss in both diagnostic categories compared with the control group. Similarly, an Australian study (1969) that compared 210 hospitalized alcoholics with controls from the population at large, matched not only for age but for sex and socioeconomic status, found parental loss to be more common among alcoholics.

Social disruption and antisocial behavior. Robins (1966) did a follow-up study of 524 children of average IQ who had been seen in a child psychiatric clinic 30 years previously. The 406 children who had been referred for antisocial behavior had a very high rate of excessive alcohol intake as adults compared with other patients and control subjects. The combined rate of sociopathy and alcoholism in their parents was surprisingly similar to that found in these subjects a generation later.

Child-rearing patterns. Rosenberg (1969) compared 3 groups of 50 individuals aged 30 or younger regarding their perception of the parenting they received; the groups had been identified as alcoholics, drug addicts, and psycho-neurotics. They were matched for age and sex. Less than half of the young alcoholics and addicts reached age 15 with both natural parents living continuously at home. The fathers of individuals in these two groups were perceived as punishing, uninterested, or rejecting; the mothers exercised little discipline. A major difference found in the neurotic group was a high incidence in the parents of disharmony and psychiatric illness, including excessive alcohol intake, but no overt social disruption; tensions were contained within the home.

McCord et al. (1960 & 1972) identified, in a Youth Prospective Study, 16 alcoholics among the boys who had been reared in intact homes and 11 of those reared in broken homes. Each was matched with a boy from the original study population who had no court conviction. The alcoholic subjects differed from the controls in that fewer of them had been reared by affectionate mothers, more had been exposed to maternal ambivalence and they had been given clear behavior expectations by their parents less often. Alcoholics from broken homes compared with those from intact homes had a higher frequency of incest or illegitimacy, maternal promiscuity, paternal deviance, maternal employment, and mutual parental role dissatisfaction.

NATURE VERSUS NURTURE: THE CONTROVERSY

The "nature versus nurture" debate regarding the etiology of alcoholism remains. There clearly is a genetic component but how this predisposition to alcoholism interacts with the environment to produce the condition is still not clear. This uncertainty is fostered by several ingredients:

(a) *The limitations of controlled designs*. Compared to the genetic studies, it is more difficult on the environmental side, to control as rigorously for the kinds of stresses within the family heightening the risk for the development of alcoholism. Factors that might contribute to a disturbed environment could include sensory deprivation in childhood, parental separation or rejection, or more subtle disturbances of the parent-child relationship. A core issue remains whether or not alcoholism itself has a specific contribution to the etiology of antisocial behavior or whether its main contribution is through its tendency to place the family in lower socioeconomic levels. Even the genetic carefully designed adoption studies do not demonstrate the effect of low socioeconomic status as adoptive parents are mostly selected for their stability, largely from a middle-class sample. Carefully designed prospective studies appear to provide the best potential vehicle for separating the different variables involved.

(b) *The relative impact of the genetic process*. The relative impact of genetic versus environmental influences may differ according to several variables such as the severity of the spectrum of illness considered. Another such factor may be the sex of the offsprings of alcoholics. A recent article by Goodwin et al. (1977) sheds further light on the relatively neglected daughter of the alcoholic. Studies of sons of alcoholics revealed a rate of alcoholism of 18%, about 4 times that of sons of non-alcoholics, whether they were raised by foster parents or by their own alcoholic parents. The incidence of alcoholism among both groups of daughters interviewed (49 adopted and 81 nonadopted) is much lower, i.e., 3–4%, although still higher than the expected rate of alcoholism for Danish women (between 0.1% and 1%). The authors speculate that daughters of alcoholics are genetically susceptible to alcoholism as are sons, but that because of cultural and possibly "counteractive biological" factors, women are more "protected" from becoming alcoholics. In addition, in the case of non-adopted daughters of alcoholics, there is an overlap of alcoholism and depression as suggested in previous work (Winokur, 1974).

(c) *The psychosocial picture of the familial versus non-familial group*. A fact remains that any population of alcoholics will have a group with a family history of alcoholism and a group without. Research is presently underway to elicit demographic and behavioral parameters differentiating these two groups (Frances et al., 1980). A sample of 7064 military men admitted to naval residential alcoholic treatment programs was categorized into a group reporting no incidence of any family history of problems related to drinking (N = 3634) and a group reporting at least one possible family member with a possible drinking problem (N = 3430). The characteristics influenced by a positive family history of alcoholism included the experience of a much less stable family environment. This group tended to be from broken homes, with larger families and with many other family members experiencing emotional problems. The familial group reported poorer academic and social performance in school, substantially more premilitary and military antisocial behavior, more severe alcohol-related physical, and psychological symptoms. Behavioral differences in familial versus non-familial alcoholics has implications for further study of the diagnosis, prognosis, prevention, and treatment of alcoholism and may shed further light on the genetic versus environmental contribution.

(d) *The variables of competence*. Most of the relevant literature on outcome predictors focusses on the casualties. Many children while suffering from their disadvantaged background are known, however, to conquer their handicap and become reasonably well-adjusted people. We recently reviewed the literature dealing with the competent offspring of psychiatrically ill parents, including alcoholics, seeking remedial clues from the analysis of their relative lack of vulnerability; once more the presence of both constitutional and environmental variables is elicited (el-Guebaly & Offord, 1980). Constitutional factors such as the child's temperament, age, sex, and intelligence are known to modify the child's experiences of parental illness.

Environmental variables also play a major role in several psychological dimensions such as the development of self-esteem, including total or nearly total acceptance of the children by their parents, clearly defined and enforced limits, and the respect and latitude for individual action that exists within the defined limits (Coopersmith, 1967). Strict parental supervision in conditions of chronic stress and poverty may be effective in preventing delinquency (Rutter, 1979). A good stable relationship with an adult has also been investigated, especially the potential position influence of the spouse of the alcoholic (Obuchowska, 1974). The perceived family environment, socioeconomic class and experiences outside the home are but some of the other related factors with a significant impact on outcome. Rutter (1979) recently emphasized the potentiating effect of stress, i.e., children subjected to one risk factor are no more likely to have a psychiatric disorder than those with none. If more than one risk factor is present, the risk for psychiatric disorder multiplies.

We studied a sample of 90 inpatients together with their spouses and children (el-Guebaly & Offord, 1980). For each consecutive admission of fifteen male and fifteen female alcoholics with a child less than age 21, a schizophrenic and a depressive parent were matched by sex, age (within five years), and time of admission. A major finding is that the characteristics of the parents, such as psychiatric hospitalizations, do not differentiate between children exhibiting high scores versus low scores on a behavioral checklist. The children with the high scores, that are more disturbed, are more likely, however, to have experienced social dislocation as measured by guardianship changes, involvement with agencies and number of moves per years of schooling.

CONCLUSIONS

Our review of predictors of outcome focussed on a number of major issues. First, there is a need for more controlled studies that take into account such variables as age, sex, education, socioeconomic class, and extent of family disorganization. The lack of prospective studies hampers efforts to tease apart the possible etiologic factors involved in producing the sequelae of being the offspring of an alcoholic. No replication of results is possible unless clear definitions of alcoholism and drinking problems, as well as other variables, are available.

Among the predictors of outcome discussed, the genetic predisposition is so far the best one available. It may be more influential near the severe end of the spectrum of alcoholism illness; it may be less so in females and it may lead to differences in symptomatology and possibly in diagnosis, prognosis, prevention, and treatment. Environmental causal links are unclear. For instance, poverty, family disorganization, alcoholism, and antisocial behavior occur together, but whether they are etiologically related (and, if so, how) has not been determined. One must however never forget that a significant group of alcoholics does not have an alcoholic parent!

This review of the dangers to the offspring of alcoholics does not mention the remedial modalities available to them. Practical prevention strategies have recently been developed in each age group; it is too early to be able to evaluate the impact of these measures on adult psychosocial outcome (el-Guebaly, 1978). Treatment approaches are also reviewed elsewhere in this publication. Alateen, which has been in existence since 1957, remains through its literature and meetings (1974), the main therapeutic resource available to the offspring of alcoholics. The cooperation between agencies concerned with the adult and those focussing on the child is still marginal with laudable efforts concentrating on family therapy as a prime component of a comprehensive alcoholism treatment program (Kamback, 1976).

It is fascinating that the growing literature on the offspring of alcoholics focusses on the casualties. Evaluation of the sources of the strengths of offspring of alcoholics should be as important as an enumeration of their potential handicaps and encompasses both constitutional and environmental influences.

REFERENCES

Alateen. *Hope for Children of Alcoholics*. Cornwall, NY: Cornwall Press, 1974.

Amark, C. A study in alcoholism: Clinical, social-psychiatric and genetic investigations. *Acta Psychiatrica Neurologica Scandinavica*, 1951, *70*, 1–283.

Bosma, W. G. H. Children of alcoholics: A hidden tragedy. *Maryland State Medical Journal*, 1972, *21*, 34–36.

Cadoret, R. J., Cain, C. A., & Grove, W. M. Development of alcoholism in adoptees raised apart from alcoholic biologic relatives. *Archives of General Psychiatry*, 1980, *37*, 561–563.

Coopersmith, S. *The antecedents of self-esteem*. San Francisco: W. M. Freeman & Co., 1967.

Cork, R. M. *The Forgotten Children: A Study of Children with Alcoholic Parents*. Don Mills, Ontario, Canada, General Publishing Co., 1969.

Cruz-Coke, R., & Varela, A. Inheritance of alcoholism: Its association with colour-blindness. *Lancet*, 1966, *2*, 1282–1284.

el-Guebaly, N. The child of alcoholic parents: A target for prevention. *ADE, Journal of the Alcohol and Drug Education Services*. Manitoba, 1978, *1*(8), 1, 14–15; 1978, *1*(9), 1, 12.

el-Guebaly, N., & Offord, D. R. The offspring of alcoholics: A critical review. *American Journal of Psychiatry*, 1977, *134*, 357–365.

el-Guebaly, N. & Offord D. R. On being the offspring of an alcoholic: An update. *Alcoholism: Clinical and Experimental Research*, 1979, *3* 148–157.

el-Guebaly, N. & Offord, D. R. The competent offspring of psychiatrically ill parents. *Canadian Journal of Psychiatry*, 1980, *25*, 457–467.

Frances, R. J., Timm, S., & Bucky, S. Studies of familial and non-familial alcoholism. I. Demographic studies. *Archives of General Psychiatry*, 1980, *37*, 564–566.

Goodwin, D. W., Schulsinger, F., Hermansen, L. et al. Alcohol in adoptees raised apart from alcoholic biological parents. *Archives of General Psychiatry*, 1973, *28*, 238–243.

Goodwin, D. W., Schulsinger, F., Moller, N. et al. Drinking problems in adopted and non-adopted sons of alcholics. *Archives of General Psychiatry*, 1974, *28*, 238–243.

Goodwin, D. W., Schulsinger, F., Knop, J. et al. Psychopathology in adopted and non-adopted daughters of alcoholics. *Archives of General Psychiatry*, 1977, *34*, 1005–1009.

Hilgard, J. R., & Newman, M. F. Early parental deprivation as a functional factor in the etiology of schizophrenia and alcoholism. *American Journal of Orthopsychiatry*, 1963, *33*, 409–420.

Kaij, L. *Alcoholism in twins*. Stockholm: Almqvist, & Wiksell, 1960.

Kaij, L., & Dock, J. Grandsons of alcoholics: A test of sex-linked transmission of alcohol abuse. *Archives of General Psychiatry*, 1975, *32*, 1379–1381.

Kamback, M. C. Family therapy in primary treatment for children and their alcoholic parents. *National Institute on Alcohol Abuse and Alcholism Information and Feature Service*, 1976, *19*, 5.

Koller, K. M., & Castanos, J. N. Family background and life: A comparative study of parental deprivation. *Archives of General Psychiatry*, 1969, *21*, 602–610.

McCord, J. Etiological factors in alcoholism: Family and personal characteristics. *Quarterly Journal of Studies on Alcoholism*, 1972. *33*, 1020–1027.

McCord, W., McCord, J., & Gudeman, J. *Origins of alcoholism (Stanford Studies in Sociology, No. 1)*. Stanford, CA: Stanford University Press, 1960.

Obuchowska, I. Emotional contact with the mother as a social compensatory factor in children of alcoholics. *International Mental Health Research Newsletter*, 1974, *16*, 2–4.

Partenen, J., Bruun, K., & Markkanen, T. *Inheritance of drinking behaviour*. Helsinki: Kaskuskirjapanio-Centraltryck-Etiett, 1966.

Rimmer, J., & Chambers, D. S. Alcoholism: Methodological considerations in the study of family illness. *American Journal of Orthopsychiatry*, 1969, *39*, 760–768.

Robins, L. N. *Deviant children grown up*. Baltimore: Williams and Wilkins Co., 1966.

Roe, A., & Burks, B. "Adult adjustment of foster children of alcoholic and psychotic parentage and the influence of the foster home," in *Memoirs of the section on alcohol studies, no. 3*. New Haven, CT: Yale University, 1945, 164.

Rosenberg, C. M. Determination of psychiatric illness in young people. *British Journal of Psychiatry*, 1969, *115*, 907–915.

Rutter, M. "Protective factors in children's responses to stress and disadvantage," in Kent, M. W., Rolf, J. E. (eds.): *The primary prevention of psychopathology: Promoting social competence and coping in children*. Hanover, NH: University Press of New England, 1979, *3*, 49–74.

Schuckit, M. A., Goodwin, D., & Winokur, G. A study of alcoholism in half-siblings. *American Journal of Psychiatry*, 1972, *128*, 1132–1136.

Sloboda, S. B. The children of alcoholics: A neglected problem. *Hospital and Community Psychiatry*, 1974, *25*, 605–606.

Winokur, G. The division of depressive illness into depression spectrum disease and pure depressive disease. *International Pharmacopsychiatry*, 1974, *9*, 5–13.

Winokur, G., Reich, T., Rimmer, J. et al. Alcoholism III: Diagnosis and familial psychiatric illness in 259 alcoholic probands. *Archives of General Psychiatry*, 1970, *23*, 104–111.

Fetal Alcohol Syndrome (FAS)—
A Review

Ian R. Holzman, MD

ABSTRACT. The deleterious effect of alcohol consumption on the developing fetus has been suspected for many centuries. It has only been during the last decade that physicians and scientists have clearly delineated the fetal alcohol syndrome and begun to investigate its causes. Children born to mothers who consume significant quantities of alcohol during their pregnancy, and especially during the first trimester, have a recognizable pattern of abnormalities. These include small size, abnormal facies, and multiple congenital anomalies. Mental retardation, behavioral problems, and poor growth are extremely common. The fetal alcohol syndrome may be among the commonest birth defects. The present goal of research efforts is to understand how and why alcohol and its metabolites interfere with the developing fetus. Scientists are also investigating the epidemiology of this unfortunate syndrome. As the consumption of alcohol increases in our society, especially among younger women, strategies for prevention and treatment are becoming increasingly vital.

Two martinis—hazardous to the unborn child? It has only been in the last decade that we have begun to realize the true implications of that question. Yet, historical reviews (Warner & Rosett, 1975) clearly indicate that both the ancient Greeks and Hebrews forbade the drinking of alcoholic beverages by women attempting to conceive. It took the indiscriminate use of gin in England during the first half of the 18th century to reaffirm the wisdom of the ancient prohibitions. Innumerable British authors throughout the 18th and 19th centuries related childhood infirmities to the consumption of alcohol during pregnancy. During the latter portion of the 19th century and the early 20th century a strong medical temperance movement developed on both sides of the Atlantic, and a number of sophisticated observations relating birth defects and alcohol were recorded. In 1901, in the rather impressively titled publication, *The Quarterly Journal of Inebriety*,

Ian R. Holzman is with the Department of Pediatrics, Division of Neonatology, at the University of Pittsburgh School of Medicine and Magee-Womens Hospital.

Bezzola published the observation that there was an increase in the number of mentally defective children born nine months after Swiss wine festivals (Bezzola, 1901).

Experimental analyses of the relationship between maternal alcohol consumption and birth defects became plentiful during the first two decades of the 20th century. A number of scientists were able to demonstrate an increased incidence of reproductive failures, birth defects, low birth weight, and a general decrease in the "vigor and vitality" of offspring. The effects were reproducible in many animal species—dogs, mice, rats, rabbits, and chickens.

The passage of prohibition in America and a general shift of interest towards the effect of environment on heredity led to a marked decrease in credible scientific investigations of the teratogenicity of ethanol. In fact, during the 1940s, many prominent scientists dismissed, outrightly, the concept that alcohol could have any effect on human germ tissue or could be the cause of any abnormality in the child. While it was accepted that damaged offspring could occur in alcoholic families, it was believed that this effect was mediated through poor nutrition and environment.

The European scientific literature continued to contain suggestive associations between alcohol and birth defects throughout the first half of the 20th century, but this concept was all but dead in the American and British literature until the 1970s. Jones and Smith (1973) published the clinical description of an apparently homogenous group of infants whose mothers were chronic alcoholics. That report rekindled a worldwide interest in the subject at a time when physicians, scientists, and the public were becoming increasingly concerned about the multiple environmental pollutants and their effect on our offspring. A flurry of reports appeared, all confirming this "new" association. Previously ignored reports, some elegant in detail, were rediscovered in the European literature. An entire field of research including metabolism, physiology, epidemiology, and sociology opened up.

CLINICAL SYNDROME

These children are, in general, born with intrauterine growth retardation—that is, they are too light and too short. They also have a significant decrease in the head circumference. There is little catchup growth; thus, these children are often diagnosed as failures to thrive during infancy. The most prominent physical abnormality, though, is a group of facial characteristics which seem to occur together and allow the syndrome to be identified or considered based on seeing the child. These facial features include hirsutism (increased hair), short palpebral fissures (distance between the inner and outer portion of the eye), epicanthic folds (an extra portion of skin over the thinner portion of the eye), a flat nasal bridge, a short, often upturned nose, a flat philtrum (the normal crease which extends between the bottom of the nose and the upper lips), a thin upper lip, and small chin (Smith, 1979). A sketch of these features is shown in Figure 1.

A number of associated congenital malformations can be seen including structural brain abnormalities; eye and ear abnormalities; cardiac, skeletal, renal, and genital defects (Clarren & Smith, 1978). The spectrum of defects can vary from children demonstrating nearly all the characteristics facial features and congenital anomalies to those with just a few deformities. Obviously the diagnosis becomes more difficult in those children only mildly affected, especially in light of the fact that none of the deformities alone are specific for the fetal alcohol syndrome. It does appear that those infants who are most severely physically affected also suffer the greatest neurological and behavioral deficits.

Mental retardation, slow development, hyperactivity, and various perceptual-motor disturbances are commonly seen in children with the fetal alcohol syndrome (Streissguth, 1977). Some of the behavioral abnormalities seen in the newborn period may also reflect an alcohol withdrawal syndrome. The average intelligence quotient of these

Figure 1

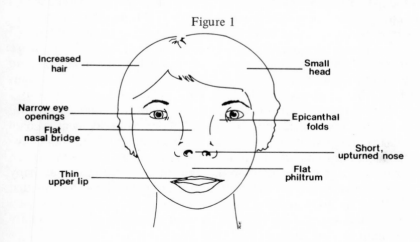

children is reported to bed in the high 60s with a wide range. Unfortunately, major handicaps persist even in the face of optimal home care and health care intervention.

PREVALENCE

I have thus far discussed the effects of alcohol consumption during pregnancy as if this were a single entity and an all-or-none phenomenon. Obviously, chronicity, quantity, and timing of consumption can all vary. Thus, while no single incidence or prevalence figures can be given, some overall estimates are available (Kline, Shrout, Stein, Susser, & Warburton, 1980). When careful prospective population studies have been made, the incidence in the general population of births varies from 1 in 400 births to 1 in 1000 births. The wide variation reflects the differences in the minimal characteristics needed to make the diagnosis as well as the prevalence of maternal alcohol consumption in different populations. Even the lowest of these estimates places the fetal alcohol syndrome as a major defect.

If we approach the epidemiologic question from the point of view of the already-identified chronically-alcoholic mother, we find an extremely high frequency of affected offspring. It would appear that at least 30 percent of the children are severely affected and 40 to 75 percent show some stigmata. Studies of these women as well as those who might not be considered chronic alcoholics have given us some idea of the relationship between quantity of alcohol consumed and the risk of bearing an affected child. It is probably fair to assume that most estimates of alcohol consumption underestimate the true amount. Nevertheless, the chances of having a child with some alcohol-induced effect (especially decreased intrauterine growth) seems to increase when the daily alcohol consumption approches one ounce of pure alcohol per day (2 martinis) while the full-blown fetal alcohol syndrome becomes very likely in mothers who drink between 3 to 5 ounces per day (6–10 martinis). Since major structural congenital anomalies are induced during the period of organ development, alcohol intake during the first three months of pregnancy should and does have the most profound effects. It is most distressing to realize that much of the damage can be done to the fetus prior to the time that many women realize they are pregnant! That is, of course, not to imply that drinking might be without effect in the latter portions of pregnancy since continued growth and development of the fetus, and especially its brain, occurs throughout pregnancy.

What can be inferred from the available research about the risks to offspring of mothers who are not chronic alcoholics but instead drink occasionally or binge drink? The answers to these questions are not clear at the present time. It would seem likely that the effects of alcohol might be most severe during the crucial early development period and that even short exposure could produce some defect. It is less obvious that infrequent social drinking in the latter stages of pregnancy is harmful, but this remains a possibility. There is some evidence that moderate alcohol consumption is a risk factor for spontaneous abortions (Kline, Shrout, Stein, Susser, & Warburton, 1980). The interaction of alcohol, even in small amounts, with other drugs such as caffeine and nicotine may also be important.

ANIMAL RESEARCH

The use of various animal models to delineate the teratogenicity of alcohol has provided important corroboration to the human syndrome. Probably the first and most important step was the identification of a pattern of deformities in a number of animals which could be ascribed to maternal alcohol consumption. Pregnancies in chickens, mice, rats, guinea pigs, and zebra fish are all affected by maternal alcoholism (Streissguth, Landesman-Dwyer, Martin, & Smith, 1980). Many defects resembling the human fetal alcohol syndrome can be seen, including developmental and behavioral effects. Dose-response curves consistent with human alcohol consumption have also been constructed. The role of nutrition can also be approached more rigorously in animal experiments by assuring adequate intake of other essential nutrients. The possibility that alcohol interferes with absorption of nutrients exists in both animal and human studies, but evidence is accumulating that alcohol (or its metabolites) is the offending agent rather than a lack of an essential vitamin or mineral.

Once it was clear that the fetal alcohol syndrome could be reproduced in animals, investigators undertook studies aimed at understanding why and how alcohol might be injurious. Alcohol and its major metabolite, acetaldehyde, freely cross the placenta. Thus, the fetus is exposed to concentrations equal to or greater than that seen in the mother. Because the fetus cannot metabolize and excrete these products as efficiently as the mother, it is likely that the concentrations are higher and remain elevated for longer periods of time. Readily achievable concentrations of alcohol in the fetus have been shown to affect protein synthesis and secretion as well as myelination of the brain (Hollstedt, Olsson, & Rydberg, 1977). Abnormal distribution of brain neurons has been demonstrated in newborn rats exposed to alcohol throughout gestation (West, Hodges, & Black, 1981). In my own laboratory, in collaboration with Dr. Stanley Fisher, we have shown that relatively brief exposure to alcohol by the rat fetus can have a profound effect on brain and liver protein metabolism (Fisher, Barnicle, Steis, Holzman, & Van Thiel, 1981).

Since alcohol is known to affect the transfer of vital nutrients into cells, an area which is just now being explored is the effect of alcohol and/or its metabolites on the transfer of nutrients to the fetus. Affected children are small and at least part of their condition may reflect a chronic state of malnutrition. Dr. Fisher and myself have had a special interest in this area and have examined the changes which occur in human placental function when exposed to alcohol. Both alcohol and acetaldehyde can interfere with the transport of amino acids to the fetus.

Future biological research will most likely focus on the metabolic and cellular effects of these toxic chemicals. Much has already been learned about the specific alterations which occur in the cell membranes when exposed to alcohol and acetaldehyde. Changes in the physical structure of cell membrane lipids as well as serious decreases in the functions of proteins and enzymes which are vital to maintenance of the function of the cell have been shown to occur. What is missing is the application of these findings to the fetal alcohol syndrome—a goal to be achieved in the near future. There is also need for more detailed investigation of the behavioral changes seen in these animal models. Much is already known but we lack strategy for overcoming learning and behavioral deficits.

STRATEGIES FOR PREVENTION AND TREATMENT

Certainly, the major goal is to prevent the occurrence of fetal alcohol syndrome. Education would appear to be the most important method for achieving this. Part of this must include an increased awareness so that active counseling before pregnancy can help prevent the use of alcohol during the early part of gestation. In those pregnancies in which abstinence is not feasible, concerted efforts to decrease consumption must be made (Rosett, Weiner, & Edlin, 1981). The role of other nutritional factors in lessening the impact of alcohol use on the fetus is an exciting area which is as yet unstudied.

As far as the child is concerned, recognition of the syndrome is essential for management. Awareness of the potential congenital anomalies can prevent unnecessary delays in diagnosis as well as undue parental anxiety. Realization that these children often fail to thrive throughout childhood allows the physician to make a diagnosis without costly hospitalization and repeated investigations. Appropriate counseling and planning for educational needs can only be accomplished if the health care team is aware of the serious problems these children may have. These considerations become especially important in light of the fact that many of these children are born into homes where alcoholism has seriously disrupted the environment. When intervention occurs the burden placed on social agencies and foster care facilities are overwhelming. Foreknowledge of the problems of these children can aid in realistic planning. It is also important to remember that increases in alcoholism in all strata of society, and especially among teenagers, may increase the prevalence of the fetal alcohol syndrome.

REFERENCES

Bezolla, D. A statistical investigation into the role of alcohol in the origin of innate imbecility. *Quarterly Journal of Inebriety*, 1901, *23*, 346–354.

Clarren, S. K., & Smith, D. W. The fetal alcohol syndrome. *New England Journal of Medicine*, 1978, *298*, 1063–1067.

Fisher, S. E., Barnicle, M. A., Steis, B., Holzman, I., & Van Thiel, D. H. Effects of acute ethanol exposure upon in vivo leucine uptake and protein synthesis in the fetal rat. *Pediatric Research*, 1981, *15*, 335–339.

Hollstedt, C., Olsson, O., & Rydberg, V. The effect of alcohol on the developing organism. *Medical Biology*, 1977, *55*, 1–14.

Jones, K. L., & Smith, D. W. Recognition of the fetal alcohol syndrome in early infancy. *Lancet*, 1973, *1*, 1267–1271.

Kline, J., Shrout, P., Stein, Z., Susser, M., & Warburton, D. Drinking during pregnancy and spontaneous abortion. *Lancet*, 1980, *1*, 176–180.

Rosett, H. L., Weiner, L., & Edelin, K. C. Strategies for prevention of fetal alcohol effects. *Obstetrics and Gynecology*, 1981, *57*, 1–7.

Smith, D. W. The fetal alcohol syndrome. *Hospital Practice*, 1979, *14*, 121–128.

Streissguth, A. P. Maternal drinking and the outcome of pregnancy: Implications for child mental health. *American Journal of Orthopsychiatry*, 1977, *47*, 422–431.

Streissguth, A. P., Landesman-Dwyer, S., Martin, J. C., & Smith, D. W. Teratogenic effects of alcohol in humans and laboratory animals. *Science*, 1980, *209*, 353–361.

Warner, R. H., & Rosett, H. L. The effects of drinking on offspring: An historical survey of the American and British literature. *Journal of Studies on Alcohol*, 1975, *36*, 1395–1420.

West, J. R., Hodges, C. A., & Black, A. C. Prenatal exposure to ethanol alters the organization of hippocampal mossy fibers in rats. *Science*, 1981, *211*, 957–959.

An Examination of Dysfunctional Latency Age Children of Alcoholic Parents and Problems in Intervention

Ellen R. Morehouse, ACSW
Tarpley Richards, ACSW

ABSTRACT. Children of alcoholic parents can develop problems in interpersonal relationships as a response to impaired parental functions. Sometimes these can be alleviated through short term supportive educative counseling. However, if the relationship style has become so impaired as to be dysfunctional, the child may need more intensive treatment. If treatment is needed, it should include the educative counseling and other ingredients common to all therapeutic intervention with children of alcoholics. In addition, the child's own behavior needs to be closely examined and interpretations need to be made to correct the faulty relationship style. Treatment with children of alcoholic parents presents a number of issues for the therapist that are not as likely to arise with children from non-alcoholic homes. These issues include the parent's role in treatment and how the drinking affects the child. By understanding how the child's problems in interpersonal relationships can be a response to impaired parental functioning, understanding how the parent's impaired functioning affects treatment, and making accurate interpretations to the child, latency age children of alcoholic parents can correct their faulty relationship styles through successful treatment.

INTRODUCTION

The characteristics that are common to most children of alcoholic parents (Cork, 1969; Morehouse, 1979), roles that they can assume (Wegscheider, 1979), and the negative impact of parental alcoholism on children (Booz & Allen, 1974; Keane & Roche, 1974; Fine, 1976;

Ellen R. Morehouse is the Director of School Programs at the Westchester Department of Community Mental Health, 148 Martine Avenue, Room 234, White Plains, NY 10601. Tarpley Richards is the Director of Family Treatment at the Kolmac Clinic, 1003 Spring Street, Suite 2, Silver Spring, MD 20910.

Haberman, 1966; Bosma, 1972; Kern, 1981; Richards, 1980; Black, 1979; Chafetz, 1971) have been well documented. A number of factors influence how a child is affected and because of these factors, some children are more adversely affected than others (Wilson & Orford, 1978). In examining the negative consequences of parental alcoholism, there is general agreement that parental alcoholism has the capacity to adversely influence the emotional, cognitive and social functions of children who are exposed over a long period of time to this parental illness. In the literature, a specific difficulty which has been mentioned repeatedly by both other investigators and adults who grew up in an alcoholic home, is unsatisfactory interpersonal relationships. It is the intent of this article to examine this observation/complaint and to point out how less than ideal parenting patterns in alcoholic caretakers affect a developing child's ability to relate with others in mutually enhancing ways.

In the first section, the authors will present a description of parental functions which are believed to be essential to a child's healthy growth and development and then will describe how alcoholism damages or destroys these functions. The next section will focus on interpersonal problems of latency age children of alcoholic parents who are seen in psychotherapy or alcohol educative counseling groups by the authors. The article concludes with a description of problems encountered by the therapist in working with these children and offers specific recommendations to mental health practitioners in confronting and working through the faulty relationship styles many of these children bring to the treatment setting.

IMPORTANT PARENT FUNCTIONS SUBJECT TO IMPAIRMENT IN THE ALCOHOLIC PARENT

Parenting styles are extremely varied. Nonetheless, there are particular parental functions that are present to a greater or lesser extent in all nuclear families. The four parental functions discussed here are selected because a parent's having varying degrees of these attributes appears to be of particular importance in understanding the child in therapy who has an alcoholic parent.

Role Stability

A child in a family needs to feel a consistent ongoing emotional relationship with the parents. This is an unconscious process. For there to be role stability there must be a consistent ongoing emotional relationship between the child and the parents, as well as a consistent emotional reaction among family members. The role specificity, i.e., who goes to the office, who cooks, who reads bedtime stories or whatever, is not as important. What does seem to be important to the child is that whatever the family roles are, they remain constant. No family can boast uninterrupted role stability. Mothers may start to work outside the home. Parents may choose to live apart and divorce. However, following these sorts of role changes, there is usually a restabilization of parental roles and the child adjusts.

In the alcoholic home, role stability is frequently replaced by role confusion, leaving the child little chance to adjust to any clear role assignment on the part of the parent. The following examples illustrate this point:

1. In a home where a mother is alcoholic, a daughter may from time to time take the place of the alcoholic wife and be cast as the confidant and love-object of the father.
2. A wife with an alcoholic husband sets the stage for the rest of the family to relate to father as an authority figure when sober, and as one of the children when drunk.

Environmental Consistency

Parents create an environmental home for their children that is conducive to caring for their young. Types of homes vary but by definition all homes should offer a place to sleep, clothing, food, and safe shelter from the weather and outside danger. Homes are usually equipped with house rules regarding these factors. For example, a child's home should offer rules as to where the child sleeps, with whom he sleeps, and when he sleeps. Clothing is provided according to the child's body and external temperature. Not only does the home offer shelter from the outside world, it also offers a safe and secure place within.

Environmental consistency in alcoholic homes has a tendency to be replaced by environmental chaos. The following clinical case illustration is presented to show the difficulties many children of alcoholic parents encounter in getting their most basic and routine needs met.

An eight-year-old boy who was presented for treatment with hyperactivity and sleep disturbance was never sure where or with whom he would sleep when bedtime did arrive. His father was alcoholic. If father was "too drunk," mother came into the child's room and ousted him from his bed and the boy was sent to another of his sibling's room to sleep in either a top bunk bed alone, a double bed with his sister or a single bed with another brother.

Dependability

A child needs to be able to count on a parent doing what the parent says he or she will do. It is unlikely that any child will survive childhood without some parental disappointment. It does happen that a parent sometime promises, for example, a trip to the zoo, only to be called away at the last minute because of an emergency at work. The average parent feels the need to follow through and does so most of the time. In alcoholic homes, disappointment in parental dependability can be alarmingly routine:

— A father stands up his son's little league championship game because he was drinking in a bar and lost track of time;
— A mother promises to take her daughter to buy a prom dress but is passed out at the time the trip was to have occurred.

Not following through on commitments and promises is especially baffling to a child when the alcoholic parent experiences a "blackout" (memory lapse while drinking). How can a parent forget something he or she definitely said or did?

Emotional Availability

Being available or being present to the child in an emotional sense is difficult to define, yet children know when this quality is absent. Alcohol interferes with a person's ability to be truly empathetic, truly giving, or truly self-denying, which are crucial ingredients to emotional availability. Chronic, heavy drinking produces an increasing self-centeredness in the user and a diminishing capacity to interact effectively with others.

As a result, when the alcoholic parent is drinking, the children's needs are often ignored. When the alcoholic parent is sober, the lack of emotional availability may continue or the parent's irritability may alternate with periods of overindulgence in an attempt to alleviate guilt over prior emotional neglect. See Figure 1.

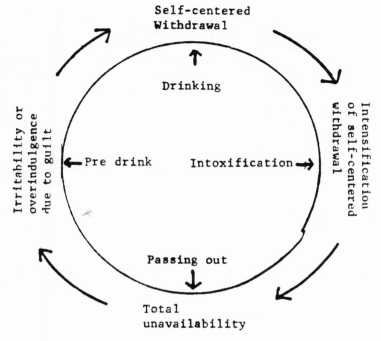

Figure 1

INTERPERSONAL PROBLEMS OF THE LATENCY AGE CHILD OF AN ALCOHOLIC PARENT

Prior to age five or six, the family is the center of the child's world. Even though children younger than this have friends, visit neighbors, stay with babysitters, and go places, the pre-school child remains primarily connected to home; the very young child does not venture far. When a child begins school, she/he is exposed on a regular basis to different adults, different values, and different expectations. The majority of children adjust to school, their first step in negotiating with the world at large. Temporary setbacks such as a displeased tone from a teacher, a fight with a new friend, can be repaired at home where the child can retreat, nurse wounds, get special attention, and prepare to return the following day. Many young children of alcoholic parents feel thrown unprepared into the world of school, or worse, they often have no place to retreat.

In addition to learning reading, writing, and arithmetic the elementary child begins to practice getting along in a social structure with others. It is in the arena of social structure and social interaction that many children of alcoholic parents have difficulty. The chart below indicates various types of interpersonal responses of children of alcoholic parents which from the author's experience seem to be related to impaired parenting patterns. The descriptions that follow indicate how the social/interpersonal response of the child results from the impaired parenting patterns of the alcoholic parents.

Parenting Pattern	Social/Interpersonal Response of the Child
1. Role instability	pseudoadult, overdependence
2. Environmental chaos	patsy, clinging, oppositional
3. Undependable	exaggeration, lying, stealing, manipulation
4. Emotional unavailability	demanding, selfish, obnoxious, withdrawing, fantasizing

Response to Parental Role Instability

The child who has experienced great fluctuation in parental role stability may feel it is unwise to be a child (dependent and needy) and the resultant behavior pattern may be pseudoadult behavior. The child may set herself/himself apart from other children and relate to them as a superior sophiscate. She/he may look down on peers for their "childishness" and have no friends as a result.

The opposite of pseudoadulthood is overdependence in which the child may be school phobic or when at school will avoid interaction with peers and find ways to cling to adults, spending a lot of time in the nurse's office with a stomachache, or sitting next to the teacher at every available opportunity.

Response to Environmental Chaos

When the child's physical environment is insecure and unstable, the youngster may try to securely attach him/herself to a group of friends or friend in such a way as to become an unwelcome permanent fixture. The child is usually viewed by these friends as a nuisance and is frequently the butt of practical jokes. The child appears willing to accept any mistreatment or will do anything to have a friend even if the child's personal safety is at risk. Another response to environmental chaos can be attempts to perpetuate this chaos in interactions with peers by being unconsciously but purposely oppositional in play. The child may intentionally ruin a game or unravel a team plan only to keep friends as off center and unsettled as she/he feels.

Response to Undependability

The child who has been repeatedly and severely disappointed by parents tends to respond by being devious in interactions with friends because a child feels the only way to get something from someone is to grab or take before the offer changes. The following example illustrates this.

> A sixth grade girl who admired a girlfriend's bicycle was told by the friend that she could ride the bicycle after school. The girl took the bicycle during morning recess and told the teacher she had permission to ride it.

Technically, the girl stole the bicycle and lied about the permission. Behind this manipulation or "conning" is an interpersonal style which is evident in many children of alcoholics who feel that in order to insure getting everything they have to set up situations in advance or take early advantage of others. Often their experience has been that to trust in others means disappointment and deprivation.

Another response to undependability can be exaggeration. Parents frequent disappointment of children can lead to feelings of worthlessness. When children feel worthless, they believe no one will like them for what they are so they exaggerate to make themselves feel they will be "worth" other children's attention and interest.

> A fifth grade boy who was promised by his father that he would be taken to a major league baseball game was disappointed because his father was severely "hung-over" and told the boy he was too sick. The boy then told all his friends that he went to the game and had dinner with his father who is best friends with the star players.

Response to Parental Emotional Unavailability

Empathy, giving, and self-denial are qualities which generally are passed on from parents to child. If the child does not receive these gifts, he or she will be hard pressed to pass them on. In addition, children who are disregarded, not listened to, and not understood by their parents, will go to great lengths to obtain these attentions from other people or they will withdraw into fantasy. Children whose alcoholic parent(s) has been emotionally unavailable may be unreasonably demanding in their relationships with peers. They may be obnoxious with teachers, worrying that if they do not go to extra-ordinary lengths to be noticed they will go unnoticed. Some of these children are totally unknowing of what is reasonable to expect from another person in terms of time and attention. In any interaction with peers the primary focus is self-centered and the goal is to constantly get for themselves. They have difficulty sharing themself and their possessions for fear that they will have to give everything and be left with nothing.

Sometimes, to avoid this hurt, they choose not to risk or assert themselves and instead prefer the safety of withdrawing into a fantasy world. For example, a nine-year-old girl often talked about, and to, her best friends who are all imaginary.

INTERVENTION WITH CHILDREN OF ALCOHOLICS

Services for children of alcoholics usually tend to be short-term supportive educative sessions that increase the child's understanding of the alcoholic and the family's reactions (NIAAA, 1981). With increased understanding many of these children experience a lessening of painful feelings (such as feelings of responsibility), feel less burdened by the alcoholism, feel less anxiety ridden and less depressed. As a result, the child's functioning usually improves.

Regardless of the modality, working with children of alcoholics usually includes the following ingredients (Richards, 1982):

— demonstrating an understanding of how children of alcoholics are affected by parental drinking
— establishing trust
— working with a child's ambivalence about discussing the parents
— giving the child an opportunity to express feelings either verbally or through play materials
— educating about alcohol and alcoholism
— helping the child develop concrete solutions for coping with the alcoholic's behavior and the child's own upset feelings
— examining the child's own behavior for the purpose of modify-ing dysfunctional behavior patterns that may have developed as a reaction to the parental alcoholism

PSYCHOTHERAPEUTIC INTERVENTION

If the child has developed dysfunctional behavior or interpersonal relationships that cause problems such as some of the examples described earlier, then the child may need more intensive treatment that focuses on helping the child to change. Treating a dysfunctional child of an alcoholic presents a number of problems and issues for the therapist that makes working with this child different from working with other dysfunctional latency age children.

Parental Issues

The most noticeable differences in treating latency age children of alcoholic parents as compared with children from non-alcoholic homes is the role of the parents. In working with children it is important to have parent involvement. The younger the child, the more crucial the involvement of the parent. The parent is needed to give a developmental history, to give an ongoing report of the child's functioning at home, and to assist in implementing the treatment plan. When a parent is actively drinking the parent is unable to be effective in carrying out these tasks.

Inaccurate Reporting

Most parents of children that are having problems feel some degree of guilt for causing or contributing to the child's problems. This is always true with the alcoholic parent who is able to identify the drinking as causing the problem. However, the actively drinking alcoholic parent utilizes denial—denial that the drinking could cause the child's problems and denial that abstinence will alleviate them. The alcoholic parent alternates between feeling guilty and being in a state of denial. As a result, she/he tends to minimize the child's problems, thereby making it difficult for the therapist to make an accurate assessment of the child in the family situation. For example, an alcoholic mother of a seven-year-old boy reported that her son did fair in first grade and got mostly Cs when he really did very poorly and got mostly Ds.

The actively drinking parent also tends to be an inaccurate reporter of ongoing events. In addition to guilt and denial, blackouts also interfere with the parent's recall.

A nine-year-old girl told her therapist she was very upset that her father did not come to visit on a weekend when he had visitation and promised to visit. The father told the therapist that he told his daughter he would be on a business trip and might not be back for the weekend.

In this situation it was hard to know if (1) the child distorted what the father had said because she wanted to see him, (2) the father promised but forgot because of a blackout and therefore really believed he never made the promise to his daughter, (3) the father distorted what was said so he would not ''lose face'' with the therapist, or (4) the father consciously decided not to see his daughter because he was too drunk and too embarrassed to call.

The parent's inaccurate reporting not only makes it difficult to make an assessment, but it also makes it more difficult to judge the child's reality testing. The more dysfunctional the child, the more difficult yet important this aspect of treatment becomes.

Overdependence on the Therapist

The alcoholic parent often feels she/he is unable to parent adequately. When the child develops symptoms/problems the parent sees this as confirmation of inadequate parenting skills and in effect tells the therapist, ''you take care of my child—I can't!'' The parent with this attitude will inappropriately want to speak with the therapist about every decision concerning the child because there is no confidence in the parent's own judgement.

Another way this is manifested is by the non-alcoholic spouse, who often feels she/he has no one to consult with because the other parent is unavailable to discuss decisions concerning the child or to provide emotional support. In this situation, the non-alcoholic spouse uses the therapist as a co-parent in place of the alcoholic. The result of these situations is more frequent phone calls and requests for appointments.

Parental overdependence on the therapist can benefit the child but it can also evoke negative counter transference because the therapist has to give more of her/himself.

Inability to Assist in Treatment

In working with young children, the parents often meet with the therapist to discuss ways the parent can assist in the child's treatment, such as waking an enuretic child to go to the bathroom, monitoring the child's intake of food, enrolling the child in activities, etc. The alcoholic parent's drinking often makes it impossible to carry out these tasks. The non-alcoholic spouse may not have dealt with his/her own angry feelings and therefore may be too emotionally needy to help the child.

> An eight-year-old boy with no friends was living with his depressed mother. The alcoholic father was living with another woman. The mother was depressed because of the husband's alcoholism and desertion. The therapist recommended that the boy be involved in after school structured activities with other boys his age. The mother didn't want him to because she wanted him home right after school to keep her company so she wouldn't be so lonely.

Inconsistent Involvement

The episodes of heavy parental drinking often cause or contribute to cancelled appointments, broken appointments, lateness, the child not being picked up on time, and non-payment of fees; all of which interfere with the child's involvement in treatment. The parent's drinking also affects the parent's involvement. As Figure 1 indicates, the parent can alternate between total non-participation and disinterest in the child's treatment while drinking, to wanting to be the ideal parent and be actively involved when not drinking.

The issue of inconsistent involvement is the most difficult, because it directly affects the child's access to the therapist. As a result, the therapist is often more reluctant to confront an alcoholic parent vs. a non-alcoholic parent because of the fear of an unpredictable response from the alcoholic that can result in the parent's removal of the child from treatment.

ISSUES FOR THE CHILD

All the issues around the parent's involvement and treatment are issues for the child. However, there are also a number of issues that the therapist must deal with directly with the child in the session. These include: (1) the child's feelings about missed appointments and lateness; (2) the child's guilt for expressing angry feelings about the alcoholic and non-alcoholic spouse; (3) the need to discuss "slips" (returns to drinking after a period of non-drinking) which come without warning and interfere with the treatment work on the child's behavior;

and (4) the intensified transference where the child sees the therapist as a parent.

The child of an alcoholic parent will typically put the therapist in the role of the idealized parent. When this happens, the child can make impossible infantile demands on the therapist to be taken care of, the child can become overly dependent on the therapist, the child can start an emotional moving away from the parent, and the child can act out the conflicts she/he has with the parents through the therapist.

These issues need to be handled carefully because they serve as the basis for the corrective emotional experience that will help repair the faulty relationship style described earlier. When a child acts out a faulty relationship style, the therapist should identify it and interpret it to the child. This should also be done when the child describes interactions with other children. The following example taken from clinical experience illustrates how this can be done.

> A ten-year-old girl constantly made unbelievable exaggerations to her friends, because she felt so worthless. As a result, her friends labeled her a liar. When describing her first quarter marks to the therapist, she reported a big improvement from last year, from Ds to As. The mother later expressed her concern for her daughter's poor grades of Cs. In the next session, the therapist was able to interpret to the girl her fear that the therapist would be disappointed by the low grades and not "like" her because she did not improve more. The girl's wild exaggeration to her friends and their dislike also provided a punishment for her angry feelings and wishes toward her alcoholic father. She felt she was a "bad girl" and therefore, deserved bad treatment from her friends.

Careful listening to the child's report of interactions, either verbally or through play, and attention to the child's interaction with the therapist provide the basis for assessment and interpretation of relationship style. Through interpretations, the child can gain greater understanding of his/her feelings and behavior and be in a stronger position to make behavioral changes.

REFERENCES

Black, C. Children of alcoholics. *Alcohol, Health and Research World*, 1979, 4(1), 23.

Booz, A., & Hamilton. *An assessment of the needs of and resources for children of alcoholic parents*. National Institute on Alcohol Abuse and Alcoholism, 1974.

Bosma, W. Children of alcoholics—A hidden tragedy. *Maryland State Medical Journal*, 1972, *21*(1), 34–36.

Chafetz, B., & Hill. Observations in a child guidance clinic. *Quarterly Journal of Studies on Alcoholism*, 1971, *32*, 687–698.

Cork, M. *The Forgotten Children*. Alcoholism and Drug Addiction Research Foundation of Ontario, Toronto, Ontario, 1969.

Fine, E. W., Yudin, L. W., Homes, J., & Heineman, S. Behavioral disorders in children with parental alcoholism. *Annals of the New York Academy of Sciences*, 1976, *273*, 507–517.

Haberman, P. Childhood symptoms in children of alcoholics and comparison group parents. *Journal of Marriage and the Family*, 1966, *28*, 152–154.

Keane, A., & Roche, D. *Developmental disorders in the children of male alcoholics*. Paper presented at the Twentieth International Institute on the Prevention and Treatment of Alcoholism, Manchester, England, 1974.

Kern, J. C., Hassett, C. A., Collipp, P. J., Bridges, C., Solomon, M., & Condren, J. Children of alcoholics: Locus of control, mental age, and zinc level. *Journal of Psychiatric Treatment and Evaluation*, 1981, *3*, 169–173.

Morehouse, E. Working in the schools with children of alcoholic parents. *Health and Social Work*, 1979, *4*(4), 144–162.

National Institute on Alcohol Abuse and Alcoholism. Services for children of alcoholics. Research Monograph *4*, 1981 (DHHS Publication No. (ADM) 81-1007).

Richards, T. Splitting as a defensive in children of alcoholic parents. In M. Galanter (ed.), *Currents in alcoholism*. New York: Grune and Stratton, 1980.

Richards, T., Morehouse, E., & Seixas, Kern, J. Psychosocial assessment and intervention with children of alcoholic parents. In *Social work treatment of alcohol problems*, 5, from the Treatment Series. New Brunswick: Publication Division, Rutgers' Center of Alcohol Studies, in press.

Wegscheider, S. The family trap. . .No one escapes from a chemically dependent family. Minneapolis, The Johnson Institute, 1976.

Wilson, C., & Orford, J. Children of alcoholics. *Journal of Studies on Alcohol*, 1978, *39*, 121–142.

Public Policy and the Child of the Alcoholic

Patricia A. O'Gorman, PhD

ABSTRACT. The child of the alcoholic as an in-need or high-risk population of a sufficiently high degree to warrant a public policy approach has been debated over the last one hundred years. This article will outline the historical development of this concept and highlight recent efforts on behalf of this group. Speculation is given as to how the proposed budget cuts will impact this group.

INTRODUCTION

In attempting to understand the direction public policy has taken in the delineation of the child of the alcoholic as an issue of concern one needs to understand the historical context into which our current concerns about alcohol problems are placed. In developing such an understanding it will become clear that our concerns of today for this group are of rather recent origin and do not necessarily represent the culmination of the "wisdom of the ages," but instead represent the outgrowth of earlier attempts to deal with a growing awareness of alcohol problems and their impact on our social order.

THE CHILD OF THE ALCOHOLIC AS AN ISSUE IN TEMPERANCE THOUGHT

Contrary to popular belief, such major social movements as prohibition had very little to do with an attempt to "save our children." Prohibition was not directed by a primary concern with youth but in the opinion of Gusfield (1973) was attempting to establish a new social order. Here power and social status moved from the hands of the wealthy into the hands of the merging middle class. As the industrial revolution spread, productivity became a major virtue. Sobriety was seen as the key of entrance into the middle class of America.

Patricia A. O'Gorman is a psychologist and consultant in private practice in East Chatham, NY.

The Women's Christian Temperance Union (W.C.T.U.) espoused two separate causes, both directed toward the urban poor. The first in essence asked the poor to emulate the behavior of the sober middle class, so that they could become more like them in other ways. The second introduced the concept of concern for the child. Such issues as promoting limits on child labor and the kindergarten campaign mark the beginning of a child focus within the alcohol issue.

As the Temperance Movement gained momentum and the horrors of intoxication became enhanced, the child as victim also became a theme. Children were portrayed as starving, and sometimes homeless, all as a result of the intoxication of the father. This became a frequent theme in Temperance Literature and in Temperance songs. It is interesting to note that no concern was given to the drinking of the adolescent. In fact, adolescents continued to be able to purchase alcohol for their parents or themselves without comment from the W.C.T.U.

The subsequent shift in public concern from alcohol problems as a productivity issue to a youth issue is not clearly documented. What can be gleaned is that youth began to be portrayed more and more as a victim of the alcohol problems of the parents and in need of protection from the parents' drinking. This developed into youth needing protection from alcohol itself. Eventually, youth moved from being seen as a victim of the alcohol use of another to an offender in terms of their alcohol use. As a result of this shift, a re-definition of what the youth and alcohol problem was occurred. This resulted in a series of laws enacted at the end of prohibition which focused on limiting the availability of the now legal use of alcohol. High on this list of new laws was the requirement for a minimum age of purchase for alcohol.

The larger society having decided that the use of alcohol by adolescents was a major problem resulted in a de-emphasis of the initial focus of the impact of parental drinking on adolescents and children. To the extent that youth and alcohol were linked as an issue, it was only concerning the extent that youthful restrictions on alcohol purchase were obeyed. Only later was there a re-emergence of this issue, and this time it concerned itself with children of alcoholics as a high-risk group.

THE ALCOHOLISM MOVEMENT

The alcoholism movement did not initially deal with the issue of the child of the alcoholic. The alcoholism movement grew in reaction to prohibition, and attempted to address the health needs of those who developed alcoholism. In the words of Marty Mann (1950), founder of the first national voluntary health association to deal with alcoholism, the National Council on Alcoholism:

> NCA was founded in 1944 in an atmosphere of almost total darkness. The word alcoholism was a taboo word. The public attitude was compounded of ignorance, fear, prejudice and hostility, and the public attitude included most professional attitudes. The "drunkard" was considered a hopeless proposition, and wholly to blame for his own condition. Almost nothing was being done about alcoholism except by alcoholics themselves (A.A.) (p. 188).

Early efforts within the alcoholism movement sought to rectify this situation, and concentrated on the delivery of health care services to the alcoholic. The preoccupation of the alcoholism field with the alcoholic can be understood in terms of their need to legitimize alcoholism as a disease. Although mention was made of the family occasionally, it was most often in regard to how they could help the alcoholic; no great efforts were directed towards their needs. Research efforts which dealt with children of alcoholics concentrated on how often this group developed the disease of alcoholism. For example, Goodwin and Guze (1974) reported retrospective studies done in 1929 and 1933 which attempted to link maternal and paternal alcoholism with the development of alcoholism in adult patients.

It was only in the 1960s that children of alcoholics began to be thought of in terms of the problems that they may develop, other than alcoholism. This population which enjoyed national attention only 50 years had been ignored. In fact, the first book written on this subject was titled *The Forgotten Children*, and published in Toronto (Cork, 1969). This book dealt with a range of emotional difficulties that children of alcoholics experience as a result of the tension of the homelife.

In 1974 the NCA created the Department of Prevention and Education. A standing committee of the Board had been created the prior year. The NCA had decided to attempt to organize the many diffuse efforts that were under way at that time. The main focus of the prevention and education efforts became children of alcoholics. In the words of O'Gorman, founder of this department, "The choice to focus our initial prevention efforts on the highest risk group, children of alcoholics, was a logical first step for a national voluntary health agency concerned first and foremost with the disease of alcoholism."

This focus was made official through a series of board policy statements. By this action NCA was placed slightly out of step with the rest of the alcoholism field who were still viewing prevention under a broad brush rubric. The push of NCA to establish target groups eventually complimented researchers in the field who sought to achieve greater specificity of desired outcomes. This new approach, called the disaggregation approach to solving alcohol problems, sought to delineate specific concerns and appropriate approaches (Room, 1974).

The National Council on Alcoholism began to stimulate the careful attention of researchers to this area by including a segment of its annual meeting devoted to this topic. In 1975, NCA held its first annual symposium on children of alcoholics. This first panel concentrated on approaches for dealing with runaway children from alcoholic homes. The following year's focus was on child abuse and neglect. A momentum has been achieved.

THE FEDERAL EFFORT

In large part due to efforts of the alcoholism movement, the federal government began to become involved in the delivery of services for those suffering from alcoholism. The 1968 amendments to the Community Mental Health Centers Act (P.L. 90-574) was the first public law specifically dealing with the treatment of alcoholism on a national basis. This was followed in 1970 by the Comprehensive Alcohol and Alcoholism Prevention, Treatment, and Rehabilitation Act (P.L. 91-616), which established the National Institute on Alcohol Abuse and Alcoholism (N.I.A.A.A.). The National Institute on Alcohol Abuse and Alcoholism, having the authority to grant research, treatment and prevention awards, and to work with major insurance carriers, quickly began to focus on the needs of children of alcoholics. In the early 1970s, N.I.A.A.A. contracted for a study on the needs and resources available for children of alcoholics (N.I.A.A.A., 1974).

Children of alcoholics were mentioned in grant announcements as specific high-risk groups suitable for prevention, early intervention, research and treatment. The importance of working with high-risk groups such as these began to emerge. The National Institute of Alcohol Abuse and Alcoholism, along with her two sister institutes, the National Institute on Mental Health and the National Institute on Drug Abuse, participated in a special grant announcement in 1979 which sought to evaluate services given to Children of Severely Disturbed Parents. The National Institute on Alcohol Abuse and

Alcoholism focused on children of alcoholics and was able to fund
two programs servicing this group: *The Student Intervention Program
in Westchester County*, a school based peer education program, and
The CASPAR Program of Cambridge, Massachusetts, a community
based peer education program. Both programs are in the process of
being subjected to extensive evaluations procedures to determine the
effectiveness of each in terms of intervening successfully with this
group.

Also in 1979, N.I.A.A.A. sponsored another first, this time a
symposium on children of alcoholics. This was the first time the
federal government had brought together a wide range of experts who
had been working in this field. The purpose of the conference and
its subsequent monograph, *Research Monograph 4, Services for
Children of Alcoholics* (1981), was in the words of the Institute Director, John DeLuca, and the Division of Prevention Director, Patricia
O'Gorman, to "serve as one step leading to increased awareness of
the issues and needs of one of our most neglected populations: children
from homes with alcoholism" (p. iii). The symposium reviewed the
gamut of available strategies from identification and early intervention to treatment and prevention. Recommendations were made to
N.I.A.A.A. and to the field of helping professionals in general in an
effort to expand the dialogue among various sectors of society who
have access to this group.

THE EMERGING DIALOGUE

The range of interests concerning children of alcoholics is certainly
expanding. An earlier publication of N.I.A.A.A., *Children In Need*,
by John McCabe (1977) is seeing renewed interest. John McCabe,
a lawyer, makes the point that children have a right to services as long
as these services do not physically alter their bodies. Although many
school districts, for example, have been reluctant to use the cases he
cites to protect themselves in offering counselling services to children
of alcoholics without parental permission, there is increasing interest
in this area.

The whole issue of how schools manage children from alcoholic
homes has been a subject of much discomfort and debate. Some programs have been set up by school districts to work with children of
alcoholics while calling the program something else and not requesting
parental permission. Others, previously mentioned, have been open
about their intent and received public funds. The National Institute

on Alcohol Abuse and Alcoholism recently contracted for the development of a resource package for professionals desirous of working with this group. The first textbook for teachers willing to teach about alcohol, appropriately called *Teaching About Alcohol* (Finn and O'Gorman, 1981), addresses how to work with this group. However, the relative lack of resources in this area remains particularly poignant. Due to the joint efforts of the N.I.A.A.A. and Blue Cross and Blue Shield, a nationwide study to determine the feasibility of offering comprehensive alcoholism benefits throughout the Blue Cross and Blue Shield System was held. This study clarified the child's right to treatment as a dependent if the parent's alcoholism is what is causing the difficulty. It is felt by those close to this study that as the insurance industry adopts more of a family coverage framework, whereby family members will have access to the physician on an out-patient basis, that this will improve the identification of health and mental health problems in the child of the alcoholic (Widem, 1981).

The prevention of intra-uterine harm to the child of the alcoholic has been a major thrust of the Fetal Alcohol Syndrome campaign soon to be released by N.I.A.A.A. Other governmental state agencies have also decided to mount campaigns, New York State's Division of Alcoholism and Alcohol Abuse being the most notable among these. The message in most of the campaigns is "the safest decision is not to drink during pregnancy." The FAS effort to date represents the government's most concerted effort on behalf of children of alcoholics.

SUMMARY

The concern for the child of the alcoholic as a public policy issue has witnessed great fluctuation throughout the last one hundred years. Given the fact that this issue is again enjoying a renewal of attention, the proposed cutback of the federal and state agencies responsible for alcohol problems will probably strike deeply into society's ability to address this issue successfully.

REFERENCES

Cork, M. *The forgotten children*. Ontario: General Publishing, 1969.
Finn, P. and O'Gorman, P. *Teaching about alcohol*. Boston: Allwyn and Bacon, 1981.
Goodwin, D., and Guze, S. Heredity and Alcoholism. In Kissin, B. and Begleiter, H. (ed.), *The Biology of Alcoholism: Clinical Pathology*. New York: Plenum Press, 1974, *3*, 37–52.
Gusfield, J. Status conflicts and the changing ideologies of the American Temperance Movement. In Pittman, D. and Snyder, C. (eds.), *Society, culture and drinking patterns*. Carbondale: Southern Illinois University Press, 1973, 101–120.

Mann, M. *Marty Mann's new primer on alcoholism.* New York: Holt, Rinehart and Winston, 1950.

National Institute on Alcohol Abuse and Alcoholism. *An assessment.* Rockville, Md., 1974.

National Institute on Alcohol Abuse and Alcoholism, Services for Children of Alcoholics. DHHS Publication N. (ADM), 81-1007, Rockville, Md., 1981.

Room, R. Governing images and the prevention of alcohol problems. *Preventive Medicine,* 1974, *3*(1): 11–23.

Widem, P. *Personal communication,* 1981.

INFORMATION SOURCES

Addiction Research Foundation (ARF)
33 Russell Street
Toronto, Ontario, Canada M5S 2S1

Alcohol and Drug Problems Association of North America (ADPA)
1001 15th Street, N.W., Room 204
Washington, D.C. 10005

American Business Men's Research Foundation
Suite 1208
Michigan National Tower
Lansing, Michigan 48933

National Center for Alcohol Education
1601 North Kent Street
Arlington, Virginia 22209

The National Clearinghouse of Alcohol Information (NCALI)
Box 2345
Rockville, Maryland 20852

National Institute on Alcohol Abuse and Alcoholism
5600 Fishers Lane
Rockville, Maryland 20852

The National Council on Alcoholism
Publications Division
733 Third Avenue
New York, New York 10017

Rutgers Center of Alcohol Studies
Publications Division
Rutgers University
New Brunswick, New Jersey 08903

Women's Christian Temperance Union
1730 Chicago Avenue
Evanston, Illinois 60201

THE MENTALLY ILL PARENT

Children of Parents Hospitalized for Mental Illness:
I. Attentional and Interactional Studies

Henry Grunebaum, MD
Bertram J. Cohler, PhD

ABSTRACT. Based on the literature regarding schizophrenia, it has been expected that aspects of attentional disorder would be communicated from parent to offspring, leading to increased vulnerability or "risk" for the development of thought disorder among such families. However, comparing groups of children of schizophrenic, depressed, and well mothers across early and middle childhood, differences, overall, across these three groups of families were less striking than had been expected, including patterns of interaction between mother and child in a structured teaching task. While evidence was found of a significant but subtle disorder of attention, greatest vulnerability consistently appeared among children of depressed mothers.

"When you have gone through that...you can never really be happy" (Bleuler, 1974).

Bleuler (1974) has suggested that the spectre of having been raised by a psychotic parent continues to cast a shadow across the life-course,

Dr. Henry Grunebaum is Director, Group and Family Psychotherapy Training, Cambridge Hospital, and Associate Clinical Professor of Psychiatry, Harvard Medical School, Cambridge, MA. Dr. Bertram Cohler is William Rainey Harper Associate Professor of Social Sciences at the University of Chicago, and an advanced candidate at the Institute for Psychoanalysis in Chicago.

even when not affecting later adjustment. Anthony (1976) has dramatically supported Bleuler's observation in his discussion of Piaget's autobiography which suggests that Piaget's mother was recurrently mentally ill. Piaget's life also dramatically demonstrates the plasticity of human development, including the capacity to overcome such early adversity as parental mental illness.

While, as genetic studies have shown, the "risk" for offspring experience of psychiatric disorder is 12 to 16 times greater than for persons not having a psychotic parent (rising to approximately 40 times as great with two psychotic parents), there is little way of predicting later status on the basis of such early experience. Less often discussed in studies of genetic risk is the majority of offspring who remain largely symptom free, yet who suffer the family and home consequences of life with a psychotic parent. Finally, it is important, as Hansom, Gottesman and Meehl (1977) note, "every high-risk sample will be genetically heterogeneous; only those children who receive the necessary genes for schizophrenia will be the true high-risk individuals" (p. 581).

What is not known at this point is the nature of those life events which precipitate the onset of psychiatric illness among those predisposed, or of factors associated with resilience or invulnerability among those offspring at risk who do not succumb (Kastenbaum, 1980). In one of the first reports focusing particularly on the issue of invulnerability, Kauffman, Grunebaum, Cohler, and Gamer (1979) review a number of cases of children who showed such invulnerability, showing superior competence at home and at school; findings from this clinical study suggested that more resilient children were able to use adult attention, were more appealing to adults, and better able to involve adults other than their "sick" parent in their lives as a kind of substitute parent.

Parental psychosis is not a unitary phenomenon, and the effects of the "major" psychoses on offspring are believed to differ in their impact upon children. For example, while there is earlier evidence that the impact of schizophrenic illness upon offspring is greater than that of depressive illness, more recent work suggests that children of schizophrenic mothers may be less seriously affected by parental mental illness, particularly when the mother shows a recurrent illness which the child can label as clearly bizarre, or when the mother is able to be relatively in contact with the child between episodes (Cohler et al., 1977; Grunebaum et al., 1978; Cohler et al., 1981).

Nature and timing of separations from the child also affect the impact of parental psychosis as does the quality of substitute care provided (Fasman, 1967). Multiple separations from a very young child, with accompanying disruptions in family functioning, will have a quite different impact from a lengthy hospitalization of the parent of an elementary school-aged child, and these from a brief hospitalization with a quick return to adequate functioning. Cowie (1961) has reported that the impact of the parental disturbance upon the child's adjustment appears to be greatest during the first months after hospitalization. If parental hospitalization is compounded by other stressful life events, if there is a disruption in continuity of care, or if the other parent has deficiencies, then the impact of the illness upon the child's development is likely to be particularly significant. Sunier and Meijers (1951) state that "the occurrence and presence of a chronic psychosis in one of the parents does not have serious consequences for the child, unless the other parent is unsatisfactory or psychiatrically ill" which is not uncommon.

Sex of the affected parent also makes a contribution to the impact of the illness upon the offspring. It is characteristic in contemporary society for the affected parent to be the mother rather than the father. Since courtship and marriage involve some degree of social assertiveness, a chronically mentally ill man is not likely to have the social skills requisite for a sustained relationship, or steady employment. Women, traditionally somewhat less active in the courtship process, may marry and have children, and succumb to mental illness during the first years after childbirth due, perhaps, to the role strain which accompanies the transition to parenthood, and which leads nearly one-quarter of all women with children of preschool age to feel depressed (Campbell, Converse & Rodgers, 1976; Weissman & Myers, 1978; Brown & Harris, 1978; Cohler, 1982).

When the father is impaired and hospitalized, it is likely that he will be extruded from the home, particularly if his behavior has been abusive towards either his spouse or his children. The family may "go on welfare," but the role of housekeeper and mother does not change. However, when the mother is hospitalized, the burdens on the father and husband are even more severe. Plagued by problems both of holding down a job and caring for the children on a minute-to-minute basis, maintaining some continuing contact with the hospitalized wife and mother, and arranging for baby-sitting and help from the extended family, all require some redefinition of the father's traditional role.

After an initial period of trying to hold the family together, and manage all expected household tasks, men in such families become depressed, and often seek divorce (Grunebaum, Gamer, & Cohler, 1981).

A final issue to be considered concerns the characteristics of the child himself. Much of the earlier literature on mental illness and the family assumed unidirectional causation from parent to the child (Lidz, Fleck, & Cornelison, 1965; Mishler & Waxler, 1968), while as early as 1905, in his Three Essays on Sexuality, Freud spoke of the "complemental series." Only recently have the systematic, empirical studies of Thomas, Chess, and Birch (1963) and Thomas and Chess (1977) shown the significance for understanding later outcome of temperamental factors. Sex of affected parent and that of offspring must also be considered. As Anthony (1971) has suggested, the child may identify with the disturbance of his parent, internalizing aspects of the parental disturbance as a part of self. Particularly since boys are often less well adjusted than girls in the period before adolescence, and are more easily upset, it is likely that the impact of parental mental illness and accompanying family disruption will be more significant for boys than for girls.

SOME FINDINGS FROM A STUDY OF MENTALLY ILL PARENTS AND THEIR CHILDREN

Many of these issues have been addressed in continuing studies of the children of mentally ill mothers carried out by the authors and their colleagues across the past two decades. In the first of these studies, a group of women was hospitalized for a psychiatric disturbance following the birth of the youngest child. When twelve such children were contrasted with twelve children of mothers never showing a psychiatric illness, on measures of cognitive development, interpersonal behavior, expression of affect, evidence of psychiatric symptoms, and overall cognitive functioning (Gallant, 1975), the children of mentally ill mothers did show greater impairment in the capacity to form interpersonal relationships, and expressed less positive affect, but did not show less overall cognitive impairment. Gallant hypothesizes that, in the absence of a stable maternal figure in whom to invest, children put all available energy into non-person oriented manipulatory activity. Since these young children aged six- to twenty-three months had resided for several months with their mothers on the wards of a psychiatric hospital, it would appear that this experience had led to enriched cognitive development, providing a growth enhancing experience similar to other group care settings such as the Kibbutz.

Finally, it should be noted that little evidence of impairment in development was found among children of mentally ill mothers hospitalized together with their mother, as contrasted with those children placed in foster care or remaining at home with multiple caretakers, traditional modes of caring for the children of mentally ill parents while their parents are in the hospital (Rice, Ekdahl, & Miller, 1971). Indeed, those children residing on the hospital wards together with their mothers showed more even performance on the developmental test measures than children not hospitalized with their mothers. In addition, the mean developmental quotient for children hospitalized with their mothers was greater than for children reared apart. The impact upon the child of joint admission of mother and child to the wards of a research oriented public psychiatric hospital is largely that of facilitating the child's cognitive development, while not affecting development in other areas.

The joint admission project was designed to evaluate efforts at improving psychiatric intervention with mentally ill mothers of young children by extending the concept of intervention from the mother as the primary patient to the mother-child unit. It was believed that, as a result of intervening with the mother and child within the milieu of the psychiatric hospital, it would be possible to support the mother in improving the effectiveness of her own mothering skills with the child as a continuing part of her life (Grunebaum & Weiss, 1975). However, as a result of changing trends in psychiatric hospitalization, including much reduced length of stay, joint admission programs have become much less practicable across the past decade. In a second study, tailored to changing trends in care of chronically mentally ill patients, a program of post-hospital nursing aftercare was developed in order to support women and their families following discharge from a state psychiatric hospital. The details of this program are described in the accompanying paper (Cohler & Grunebaum, 1981). Suffice to say here that a group of 50 women and their children was followed over several years following discharge from a cooperating state psychiatric hospital. The mothers were mainly seriously and chronically ill people. Children in these families were studied intensively using both measures of intellectual and social development across the first five years of life (Bayley scales; Stanford-Binet; Wechsler Primary and Preschool Scale), administered at the time of the mother's entrance into the study and, again, at termination of participation, as well as a number of specific measures of cognitive and social development administered at "landmark" birthdays (ages one, three, and five, to correct for the confounding effect of age).

Since the capacity to sustain and deploy attention has been highlighted in much research, especially in schizophrenia, across the past two decades as a major indicator of impairment in psychological development among the children of mentally ill parents (Gunderson, Autry, & Mosher, 1974; Garmezy, 1978), particular effort was expended on the assessment of this aspect of the child's cognitive functioning. A first effort to examine this assumption was made with the children reaching their third birthday, using a measure of selective attention (Children's Embedded Figure Test (EFT), Gamer et al., 1977) in which the child must "disembed" or separate a particular stimulus figure from an interfering background, and a measure of sustained attention, or concentration, in which the child must respond to a particular stimulus presented in the viewing window of a rotating drum (Continuous Performance Task, Herman et al., 1977).

Unfortunately, the number of children in the three-year-old group is so small that it has been difficult to examine differences within the group of mentally ill mothers and children separately according to diagnosis. While children within the mentally ill group did indeed show greater impairment in selective attention (Gamer et al., 1977), an analysis-of-variance carried out by this investigator shows that such impairment is apparent primarily on the more difficult stimuli late in the series when, presumably, the children are tired. These children show a subtle but real deficit. Further, when examining the scores of the ten children with the greatest difficulty, seven of them have depressed rather than schizophrenic mothers.

The greater risk for impairment in attention among these children of depressed mothers becomes apparent in a study of the children in the five-year-old group (Cohler et al., 1977), who showed significantly greater impairment than children either of schizophrenic or well mothers, whose scores on the measure of selective attention were not differentiated. Perhaps even more striking, the children of depressed mothers show not just statistically lower scores on the WPPSI, but clinically relevant scores as well, with differences between children of depressed and children of schizophrenic and well mothers exceeding 10-12 points. We believe that it is the apathetic withdrawal of these depressed mothers which has had such a profound impact on their children's development. Perhaps it is better to have a mother whose actions are clearly bizarre, and can be labeled as such, than a mother whose behavior is not so obviously inappropriate and whose symptoms can be more easily tolerated by society, but whose impact on their children is more clearly deleterious and whose children also have more accidents and emergency room visits. Finally, it should be noted that the groups of children used in the present research are so small that these results should be regarded as tentative, to be confirmed through further systematic study of the children of schizophrenic, depressed, and well mothers.

A follow-up study of the mothers and children studied earlier in the Aftercare research was attempted. Unfortunately, it was difficult to locate a number of these families without the efforts of an intervention project which helped the family to remain intact and involved with the research. But approximately half of the mothers in the mentally ill group, and relevant "controls" in the well group (41 percent of mentally ill mothers and 45 percent of well mothers), could be located at the time of the follow-up research.

The number of children tested at any given landmark birthday in the earlier research was too small for any systematic study of change over time using the original measures. And rather than use only the original instruments, the previously administered measures of selective and sustained attention were used, supplemented by more recently developed measures of related cognitive functions, including leveling-sharpening (Santostefano, 1978), and present school adjustment both as reported by parents, using a modification of the Rochester Adaptive Behavior Interview (RABI) designed by Jones (1977) and an interview designed especially for the present study of the children's report of present functioning in school and at home.

Findings concerning the children's cognitive development very much parallel our earlier findings concerning selective and sustained attention (Grunebaum, Cohler, Kauffman, & Gallant, 1978). Comparing the boys and girls of schizophrenic, depressed, and well mothers, the boys of the depressed mothers show greatest impairment of the Embedded Figure Test (EFT), with the difference most apparent on the most difficult series of stimuli. Children of depressed mothers, including both boys and girls, make more errors on the Continuous Performance Task (CPT) than children of schizophrenic mothers. What is also striking about these results is that, in their cognitive performance, the children of schizophrenic mothers very closely approximate the children of well mothers. Indeed, on the measure of intelligence (WISC), where there are no longer differences between the three groups of children, the scores of the children of schizophrenic mothers closely approximate those of well mothers, with the scores of children in the depressed group some 8 points lower for the group as a whole, not statistically significant, but still consistent with the earlier study of five-year-old children.

Differences in social development are less notable than those regarding cognitive functioning. Depressed mothers rate their children's adjustment overall as less successful than mothers in the two other groups, but this interview data is clearly affected by the mother's disturbance which leads to increased feelings of unworthiness regarding both self and significant others. Children of depressed mothers spend more time alone and have fewer friends than children of schizophrenic mothers, while children of schizophrenic mothers reported conflict at home and family problems to a greater extent than children of depressed mothers, and both groups of children report an adequate adjustment at school. This follow-up study raises a number of interesting questions. Once more, the children at risk or who appear to be most vulnerable are the children of the depressed mothers, about whom much less has been written, and not, as expected on the basis of earlier findings and theoretical assumptions regarding the transmission of mental illness, the children of schizophrenic mothers.

Additional study of the children of depressed mothers may reveal a degree of vulnerability not previously recognized among such children. It is also possible that the effects of schizophrenia on the child's functioning will not become apparent until adolescence when the child is required to engage in a more complex and differentiated set of social relations and must be more able to "take the role of the other," and to function in the complex ways expected of adults in our society. It is possible that the effects of depression on the child's development are noticeable early in the child's life, diminishing in importance by adolescence, while the effects of schizophrenia on the child's development are delayed, not appearing until adolescence. The only data relevant to this hypothesis come from a pilot study we carried out on schizophrenic women and their children aged 13–14. Using a measure of role taking based on Feffer's (1966) technique for assessment of role taking, and a unique behavioral measure of ability to take the role of the other in which mother and child sit back-to-back at a checkerboard with objects in different squares, varying systematically either in shape or color and in ambiguity (Glucksberg & Krauss, 1967; Glucksberg, Krauss, & Weisberg, 1966), reconciling the two boards so they are alike, children of schizophrenic mothers show significantly greater difficulty in role taking, particularly in the checkerboard task, than children of well mothers matched for age, sex, and level of intellectual functioning. This measure has not been tried with depressed mothers and their children of the same age, but clearly, the extension of this study to include depressed mothers and their adolescent children is a task of some importance.

We also have done interaction studies with five-year-old children of psychotic mothers. The interaction task utilizes an adaptation of the Picture Arrangement subtest of the Wechsler Intelligence Scale for Children (WISC). The mother is first asked to arrange four sets of pictures, one set at a time, so that they tell a story, and to tell the story to her child. She is asked to explain to her child what she is doing "so that he will understand and be able to do it by himself." The child is then asked to arrange the four sets his mother has already done plus five new sets. He is asked to tell his mother the story, and the mother is instructed to feel free to assist the child if he appears to need help "so that he will be able to understand and do it by himself." The sets of pictures selected are easily done by most mothers, as determined by pretesting. They were graded in difficulty, however, so that while most are easy for five- and six-year-old children, some are not.

The interaction is tape-recorded and transcribed. The transcript is then coordinated with a written record of nonverbal interactions which an observer has made during the session. The protocols may be scored for a wide variety of operationally defined behaviors of both participants, such as: attentional focusing, clarification and facilitation of task, appropriate and inappropriate motivating, reinforcement, positive and negative emotional expression and communication difficulties.

The findings for the group of five-year-olds and their parents are as follows. Examining such factors as the nature of positive and negative affect expressed while completing the task, the speed with which the task was completed, the number of inferences made by mother and child while working on the task, and evidence of communication problems, all codes showing satisfactory reliability, there are no variables differentiating the groups of schizophrenic, depressed, and well mothers and their children. Not only do the differences fail to reach generally accepted significance levels, the best conclusion would be that there are no differences either in success of task completion, affect expressed, or evidence of communication difficulties between mother and child for any of these tasks. Within the schizophrenic group, but not within the depressed or well groups, children who are more successful in following the mother's instructions have mothers who report more positive affect. There is little evidence that maternal performance on measures of selective and sustained attention is related in any meaningful manner to the child's performance in the interaction task, although mothers showing a greater impairment in selective attention (errors or failures) show greater communication difficulties, within the groups both of schizophrenic and well mothers.

It is possible that the interaction task failed to measure critical aspects of the mother's relationship with the child and, as noted also for the interaction study among three-year-olds and their mothers, that performance at home differs from that in the laboratory. The complete absence of positive findings across two separate investigations of mother-child interaction can also be regarded as suggesting that the mother's relationship with her child, particularly in a complex structured teaching task, is not adversely affected by her disturbance. Whatever the impact of the mother's illness upon the child's cognitive development, this influence is more subtle than might at first be assumed.

At the same time, a number of these children appear unusually resilient in the face of enormous adversity, including multiple separations from their mother, continuing maternal psychopathology, and quite often, accompanying disruptions due to divorce or separation in the relationship between the parents. A number of these children, particularly with schizophrenic mothers, appear to be able to use substitute adults, and to compensate for family difficulties by becoming invested in activities outside the home, hobbies, and school work. These children, termed "superkids" by Kauffman et al. (1979) function even more effectively than children of well mothers, demonstrating once again the inherent plasticity in human development and the lack of predictability of development over time.

It is possible that results such as those reported in this paper, focused primarily upon children from birth through middle childhood, do not include a sufficient scope of the life-course to encompass the most vulnerable years. Adolescence and young adulthood may provide a new set of developmental tasks which will reveal psychopathology not so readily apparent during early childhood. What emerges from the present set of studies is some evidence of increased vulnerability in subtle aspects of cognitive processes which does not appear presently to affect overall functioning of most of these children of mentally ill mothers.

SUMMARY AND CONCLUSION

A series of studies are summarized regarding the cognitive and social development of such children from infancy through middle childhood, based on families treated in a series of intervention projects. Overall, these studies reveal less psychopathology among children of recurrently mentally ill mothers than would have been expected. Further, although current socialization models would suggest that children of schizophrenic mothers would be particularly vulnerable as a consequence of transmission of deviant thought processes across generations, children of depressed mothers show greatest vulnerability on measures of intellectual functioning and of attention. Maternal withdrawal and lack of affect appears to be particularly detrimental for the child's development, while children of schizophrenic mothers show cognitive and social skills through middle childhood not notably distinguished from their well counterparts. Ironically, the most competent children have recurrently schizophrenic mothers; these children appear to have been able to selectively ignore maternal psychopathology and to take advantage of other adults as caretakers and teachers during periods of increased maternal psychopathology. Such findings point to the importance of understanding issues of resilience and invulnerability, as well as of vulnerability, and to consider these issues in a life-course context.

REFERENCES

Anthony, E. Folie a deux: A developmental failure in the process of separation-individuation. In J. McDevitt and C. Settlage (Eds.), *Separation-individuation: Essays in honor of Margaret S. Mahler*. New York: International Universities Press, 1971, 253–273.

Anthony, E. How children cope in families with a psychotic parent. In E. Rexford, L. Sander, and T. Shapiro (Eds.), *Infant psychiatry: A new synthesis*. New Haven: Yale University Press, 1976, 239–250.

Baldwin, A., and Baldwin, C. The study of mother-child interaction. *American Scientist*, 1973, *61*,714–721.

Brown, G., and Harris, T. *Social origins of depression: A study of psychiatric disorder in women*. New York: Free Press-Macmillan, 1978.

Bleuler, M. The offspring of schizophrenics. *Schizophrenia Bulletin*, 1974, No. 8, 93–107.

Campbell, A., Converse, P., and Rodgers, W. *The quality of American life: Perceptions, evaluations, and satisfactions*. New York: Russell-Sage, 1976.

Cohler, B. Parenthood, psychopathology, and child-care. In R. Cohen, B. Cohler, and S. Weissman (Eds.), *Parenthood and parenting as an adult experience*. New York: Guilford Press, 1982.

Cohler, B., Gallant, D., Grunebaum, H., Weiss, J., and Gamer, E. Disturbance of attention among schizophrenic, depressed, and well mothers and their young children. *Journal of Child Psychology and Psychiatry*, 1977, *18*, 115–135.

Cohler, B., Grunebaum, H., Kauffman, C., and Gallant, D. Social adjustment among schizophrenic, depressed, and well mothers and their school-aged children. In H. Morrison (Ed.), *Children of depressed parents*. New York: Grune and Stratton, 1981.

Cowie, V. The incidence of neurosis in the children of psychotics. *Acta Psychiatrica Scandinaca*, 1961, *37*, 37–87.

Fasman, J., Grunebaum, H., and Weiss, J. Who cares for the children of psychotic mothers. *British J. Psychiatry*, 1967; *9*(2), 84–99.

Feffer, M., and Suchotliff, L. Decentering implications of social interaction. *Journal of Personality and Social Psychology*, 1966, *4*, 415–422.

Firth, R., Hubert, J., and Forge, A. *Families and their relatives: Kinship in a middle-class sector of London*. New York: Humanities Press, 1970.

Freud, S. Three essays on the theory of sexuality (1905). *Standard Edition*. London: Hogarth Press, 1953, *7*, 130–243.

Gallant, D. Children of mentally ill mothers. In H. Grunebaum, J. Weiss, B. Cohler, D. Gallant, and C. Hartman, *Mentally ill mothers and their children*. Chicago: The University of Chicago Press, 1975, 177–233.

Gamer, E., Gallant, D., Grunebaum, H., and Cohler, B. Children of psychotic mothers *Archives of General Psychiatry*, 1977, *34*, 592–597.

Gamer, E., Grunebaum, H., Cohler, B., and Gallant, D. Children at risk: Performance of three-year-olds and their mentally ill mothers on an interaction task. *Child Psychiatry and Human Development*, 1977, *8*, 102–114.

Garmezy, N. Attentional processes in adult schizophrenia and in children at risk. *Journal of Psychiatric Research*, 1978, *14*, 3–34.

Glucksberg, S., and Krauss, R. What do people say after they have learned how to talk? Studies of the development of referential communications. *Merrill-Palmer Quarterly*, 1967, *13*, 309–316.

Glucksberg, S., Krauss, R., and Weisberg, R. Referential communication in nursery school children: Method and some preliminary findings. *Journal of Experimental Child Psychology*, 1966, *3*, 333–342.

Grunebaum, H., Cohler, B., Kauffman, C., and Gallant, D. Children of depressed and schizophrenic mothers: Findings from a follow-up study. *Child Psychiatry and Human Development*, 1978, *8*, 219–228.

Grunebaum, H., Gamer, E., and Cohler, B. The spouse in depressed families. In H. Morrison (Ed.), *Children of Depressed Parents*. New York: Grune and Stratton, 1981.

Grunebaum, H., and Weiss, J. Planning for joint admission. In H. Grunebaum, J. Weiss, B. Cohler, D. Gallant, C. Hartman, *Children of Mentally Ill Mothers*. Chicago: The University of Chicago Press, 1975, 4–82.

Gunderson, J., Autry, J., and Mosher, L. Special report: Schizophrenia, 1973. *Schizophrenia Bulletin*, Summer, 1974, 15–54.

Hanson, D., Gottesman, I., and Meehl, P. Genetic theories and validation of psychiatric diagnoses: Implications for study of children of schizophrenics. *Journal of Abnormal Psychology*, 1977, *86*, 575–588.

Herman, J., Mirsky, A., Ricks, D., and Gallant, D. Behavioral and electrographic measures of attention in children at risk for schizophrenia. *Journal of Abnormal Psychology*, 1977, *86*, 27–33.

Hess, R., and Shipman, V. Early experience and the socialization of cognitive modes in children. *Child Development*, 1965, *36*, 869–886.

Hess, R., and Shipman, V. Cognitive elements in maternal behavior. *Minnesota Symposium on Child Development*, 1967, 1.

Jones, F. The Rochester adaptive behavior inventory: A parallel series of instruments for assessing social competence during early and middle childhood and adolescence. In J. Strauss, H. Babigian, and M. Roff (Eds.), *The origins and course of psychopathology: Methods of longitudinal research*. New York: Plenum, 1977, 249–281.

Kastenbaum, C. Children at risk for schizophrenia. *American Journal of Psychotherapy*, 1980, *34*, 164–177.

Kauffman, C., Grunebaum, H., Cohler, B., and Gamer, E. Superkids: Competent children of psychotic mothers. *American Journal of Psychiatry*, 1979, *136*, 1398–1402.

Lidz, T., Fleck, S., and Cornelison, A. *Schizophrenia and the family*. New York: International Universities Press, 1965.

Mishler, E., and Waxler, N. *Interaction in families: An experimental study of family processes and schizophrenia*. New York: John Wiley and Sons, 1968.

Santostefano, S. *A biodevelopmental approach to clinical child psychology: Cognitive controls and cognitive control therapy*. New York: John Wiley, 1978.

Sunier, A., and Meijers, N. A. The influence of a chronical (sic) psychosis of one of the parents upon the development of the child. *Folia Psychiatry*, 1951, *54*, 323.

Thomas, A., Chess, S., Birch, H., Hertzig, M., and Korn, S. *Behavioral individuality in early childhood*. New York: New York University Press, 1963.

Thomas, A., and Chess, S. *Temperament and development*. New York: Brunner/Mazel, 1977.

Weissman, M., and Myers, J. Rates and risks of depressive symptoms in a United States urban community. *Acta Psychiatrica Scandinaca*, 1978, *57*, 219–231.

Children of Parents Hospitalized for Mental Illness:
II. The Evaluation of an Intervention Program for Mentally Ill Mothers of Young Children

Bertram J. Cohler, PhD
Henry Grunebaum, MD

ABSTRACT. Findings are reported from a clinical research project developed to intervene in the pattern of recurrent rehospitalization characteristic of a group of pervasively disturbed mothers of young children. Families in which mothers were visited by specially trained psychiatric workers on a weekly or more frequent basis were compared with those in which mothers were seen only infrequently, and a group of well families in which the wife and mother had never sought psychiatric assistance. While few findings appeared between the maximally and minimally treated groups, across these two groups of mentally ill mothers, women hospitalized more often were less able to differentiate between their own needs and those of their children, and showed both greater life-event stress, and more active conflict with the maternal role.

The development of psychiatric illness among mothers of young children presents a dilemma both for family and society. As Rice, Ekdahl, and Miller (1971) have shown, psychiatric hospitalization leads to a disruption of the family system, resulting in multiple separations for children at home and uncertain patterns of child-care, as well as continuing disruptions from marital strains associated with disturbance and hospitalization. While recognizing that hospitalization presents problems for the whole family, the hospital may assume that

Dr. Bertram Cohler is William Rainey Harper Associate Professor of Social Sciences at the University of Chicago, and an advanced candidate at the Institute for Psychoanalysis in Chicago. Dr. Henry Grunebaum is Director, Group and Family Psychotherapy Training, Cambridge Hospital, and Associate Clinical Professor of Psychiatry, Harvard Medical School, Cambridge, MA.

the mother alone is the primary patient. All too often the patient's social history does not even show that she is a mother or how many children she has and their ages; hospitals fail to recognize that this failure to include the whole family as the identified patient interferes in the rehabilitation of the wife and mother. Although troubled, mentally ill mothers do feel a continuing responsibility for their children. When alternative arrangements are unstable, involving temporary foster placements or substitute childcare by resentful relatives, the burden of worry and guilt which the mother experiences further compounds her psychiatric distress.

Problems associated with hospitalization are compounded among those families in which the mother's illness is a recurrent one, with periods of increased stress, often idiosyncratically defined, associated with exacerbation of symptoms, leading to rehospitalization. As women are rehospitalized, the coping resources of the larger family unit become exhausted. The family becomes increasingly less able to resolve problems associated with the mother's illness, increasing the impact of this illness upon children and spouse. Relatives are less willing to help with the childcare, and even social agencies tire of providing makeshift resources on a continuing basis. All too often, as the mother repeatedly returns to the hospital, the husband becomes discouraged, believing that little progress is possible in terms of the rehabilitation of the wife and mother, leading to attempts to dissolve the marriage (Grunebaum, Gamer, & Cohler, 1981).

To date, there have been few programs addressing the issue of the rehabilitation of the mentally ill mother. Based on a pioneering program at the Cassel Hospital in Great Britain (Main, 1958), in which the entire family was brought into the hospital when the mother became psychiatrically impaired, a program was begun in the United States in which mentally ill mothers were admitted jointly to the wards of a research-oriented state mental hospital together with their children between the ages of six and twenty-four months (Grunebaum & Weiss, 1975). Central to this program was the view that the presence of the baby on the ward would provide a unique opportunity to intervene in such a manner as to support the mother's skills by helping her to learn to care for her baby under the direction of the ward nursing staff while, at the same time, increasing the salience of the mothering role as an issue in the mother's individual psychiatric treatment. This program, which subsequently was replicated in a large state hospital, demonstrated that joint admissions could facilitate the mother's rehabilitation, increasing her own awareness of her role as mother (Van Der Walde et al., 1968).

This pilot program did not provide a systematic evaluation of outcome for the mother and her family. Further, as changing patterns of hospitalization during the past two decades have emphasized community care rather than hospital treatment, there has been less need for the kind of program represented by the joint admission procedure. The length of time required to negotiate the joint admission, including preparatory work with the nursing staff and the mother's psychiatrist, and the demands for staff involvement, both suggest that other methods must be developed to provide support for the formerly hospitalized mother as she struggles to meet her many conflicting adult responsibilities.

It was in an attempt to provide such support for these formerly hospitalized mentally ill mothers and their families that a second intervention program was formulated by the present authors and a group of colleagues in order to provide community care which might both facilitate the mother's adjustment, and prevent rehospitalization, which has such a dramatic impact upon the adjustment of the entire family unit.

With the assistance of a grant from the Division of Applied Research of the NIMH, home visits by specially trained psychiatric nurses were provided for 50 formerly hospitalized psychotic mothers who had at least one child below age six, recruited from participating public and private psychiatric hospitals in the Boston area and who volunteered to participate. The intervention was offered for either one or two years. In order to provide a relatively stringent test of the effects of treatment, the study was designed to include three groups of mothers. Two groups of 25 were formed by random assignment of the psychotic mothers. One of these groups received intensive long-term nursing aftercare while the other group received minimal contact. A third group of mothers with no psychiatric history, obtained through advertisement in local papers, was individually matched to the mothers in the other two groups on social class, ethnicity, parity, and age and sex of the youngest child. These mothers did not receive the intervention. In all instances, psychiatric home-nursing aftercare was not in lieu of, but rather in addition to, other services the families were receiving.

The intervention consisted of weekly home visits lasting between 1 and 1½ hours and focused, in particular, on the mother's relationship with her youngest child. Since the mother was seen in her home, her interactions with her children could be directly observed and discussed. The effects of the psychotic experience and unresolved issues in the mother's own life were also important subjects. While the two high-risk groups did not differ in other treatment parameters such as the use of drugs or other treatment, the intensive treatment group received 1384 home visits while the minimally treated group was visited 130 times.

At the time of admission to the study and at termination of the intervention a series of assessments of the mother and her youngest child were made. These included, for the mother: the Minnesota Multiphasic Personality Inventory (MMPI), a social-role performance evaluation interview, and a clinical interview of both the mother and her husband when he was willing. The child was administered an age-appropriate intelligence test. Ratings were made of the child's behavior, affect, and social interactions during the testing. Child psychiatric evaluations were also carried out.

The two treatment groups were well matched. The majority of the women were lower middle-class, in their late 20s, chronically psychotic, usually diagnosed schizophrenic, and functioning rather poorly. Comparisons of women within the two mentally ill groups at the time of termination showed no significant differences in diagnosis, chronicity, or duration of hospitalization.

Overall, there are fewer noticeable changes between the intensive and minimally treated groups than had been expected in advance. The failure to observe striking differences between intensively and minimally treated patients may, in part, arise from the fact that the intensively followed patients continued to see their nurses at least weekly, and sometimes more often, for as crises arose within these families, the nurses intervened not by seeing these patients directly but, rather, by referring them to the appropriate community agencies. However, much effort was required in order to be sure that a woman received the appropriate treatment and that the referral source followed up on the initial visit.

The effect of these contacts was to minimize the differences between the treatment offered to the intensive and minimally followed groups. Since the very act of placing a patient in a "waiting list" control group has been shown to have therapeutic effects, even minimal contact with the nurse had an advantageous effect. Furthermore, knowledge that the nurse was available in time of crisis was also a source of emotional support for these minimally treated women.

Consistent with this overall conclusion of a few differences between the intensively and minimally followed groups, it should be noted that the mean number of rehospitalizations during the study does not differentiate women in the two groups. The mean number of rehospitalizations for former patients during the study period was 1.95 (standard deviation of 1.30) while for the minimally treated group, the mean was 2.05 (standard deviation of 1.34). Thus, patients were about as likely to be rehospitalized if they were seeing a nurse on a weekly basis as they were if the intervals between visits were less frequent. However, rehospitalization, itself, is a difficult criterion to use since the decision that a woman should return to the hospital may be a "therapeutic" one. For example, as a woman begins to explore her own problems, she may experience a period of marked upset, at which point it may be agreed that she would experience feelings of greater safety from being in the hospital.

Turning to the more specific data on the two groups of intensively and minimally followed mothers, the former patients' own reports of their experiences on the project are disparate from data obtained either from the self-report questionnaire measures or that obtained from coding the semi-structured interviews with these women regarding their social role functioning. The following differences between the intensive and minimally followed mothers are significant at less than the .05 level: a greater feeling of value as a result of having participated on the project, a greater sense of being able to solve one's own problems, a greater sense of having received help as a result of contact with the nurse, a feeling of being more able to think through one's own problems, as a result of nursing interventions, improvement in one's capacity to care for one's own children and to respond affectionately to one's husband, and an ability to achieve more satisfactory relationships with one's own parental family.

Comparing the husbands' reports of these intensively and minimally treated women, there were relatively few differences between the groups that even approach the conventional .05 significance level. While the husbands of the intensively treated women found the program of greater use (p = .001), these husbands did not report that their wives functioned any better than was reported by the husbands in the minimal treatment group.

From the point of view of social role functioning, ratings of the social role interviews concur with the evaluations made by the patients' husbands. Overall, at the conclusion of the project, there were few differences between the social role performance of the intensively and minimally treated women. Similar results obtained when considering self-reported psychological distress on the MMPI. None of the thirteen scales reveal any differences between these two groups of women at the termination of the project.

Perhaps the model for evaluating change in psychotherapy should be based on that of consumer satisfaction. Judged from this perspective, the patients in the intensively followed group of mothers felt they got more out of the project and were more satisfied both with the project and with their own inner changes during the period of the project than was true for the women in the less intensively followed group. However, from any outside perspective, the differences were less clear.

Nurses were asked to rate the presence of change in six different areas of functioning during the period of nursing intervention: (1) capacity for closeness as friend and neighbor; (2) adaptive functioning in housewife role; (3) freedom from disruptive psychological symptoms; (4) resolution of intra-family conflicts; (5) capacity for closeness with husband; and (6) capacity to work towards the solution of psychological conflicts. These dimensions were found to be intercorrelated and were summed to create a single global rating of change in functioning over the intervention period.

In order to determine the inter-rater reliability of this rating of change, the project co-director responsible for supervision of the nurses independently rated the extent of change in these patients across the intervention period. The resulting correlation ($r = .776$, $p = .001$) shows that psychiatric nurses could reliably rate the amount of change observed in their patients across the study period.

Contrasting the two groups of patients on these scales, five of the seven scales showed improvement favoring intensively treated mothers, including the capacity to function as friend and neighbor ($p = .01$), capacity to function as housewife ($p = .05$), freedom from symptoms ($p = .02$), capacity for closeness with husband ($p = .03$), and the summary global change index ($p = .02$). While these ratings provide some evidence that women in the intensively treated group showed greater improvements, the fact that the psychiatric nurses knew the study hypotheses and were aware of the treatment group to which their patients belonged leads to the possibility that their ratings may have been biased in the direction of the more intensively treated patients.

Another way these ratings may be used is in the study of the correlates of improvement across both the intensively and minimally treated groups, where we may ask what relationships exist between these ratings of change and other aspects of patients' psychological and social functioning. In studying this relationship, correlations significant at the .05 level or less were found betwen nurses' global ratings of change over the period of the study and independent data regarding both psychological and social functioning among these formerly hospitalized mothers. Patients across the two groups rated as having changed more were also less chronically disturbed (r = .498, p = .01), showed a shorter period of onset of symptoms prior to hospitalization (r = .373, p = .05), fewer rehospitalizations over the course of the study period (r = .495, p = .01), and a significantly greater improvement in all role relationships with the exception of that as daughter.

Patients rated as changing more also showed more adaptive attitudes on the attitude factors of encouraging mother-child reciprocity (r = .387, p = .05), and fostering appropriate mother-child closeness (r = .498, p = .01). Ratings of greater change were correlated with less feeling of depression and poor morale on the MMPI (r = .504, p = .01), fewer psychotic symptoms (r = .386, p = .05), less manifest hostility towards others (r = .348, p = .05), and conflict with authority (r = .316, p = .05). Women rated as changing more were those with less stress both in their own lives (r = .358, p = .03) and their husbands' lives (r = .408, p = .01). Women rated as changing more over the course of the study were more likely to report that the nurse had helped them to think about their problems (r = .325, p = .05), to be better able to perform as housewife (r = .405, p = .01), wife (r = .305, p = .05), and mother (r = .420, p = .01), to experience fewer hallucinations and other psychotic symptoms (r = .339, p = .05), and to feel closer to their husbands (r = .334, p = .05). Ratings of greater change were also associated with husbands' reports of greater changes in their wives' home adjustment (r = .400, p = .01), and with greater feelings of satisfaction with the nursing project (r = .394, p = .05).

Overall, across these two groups of more and less intensively treated former patients, women whose premorbid adjustment is less chronic, who show a greater capacity for investment in interpersonal relationships, who are able to function more adequately as wife and mother, and who have experienced less stress in their own lives, are more able to profit from intensive nursing aftercare. Associated with greater change, nurses treating such women report greater feelings of optimism and usefulness for the patient. Finally, it should be noted that these feelings towards the patient are by no means simply stereotypes maintained throughout the period of the study. There is no relationship between the nurses' ratings of their subjective reactions towards patients at the beginning and end of the study. Across fourteen of the fifteen scales of therapist's subjective reactions towards the patient, only for the scale of Difficulty in Terminating Individual Contacts is there a significant correlation ($r = .423$, $p = .01$) between initial and terminal ratings. Nurses change their subjective reactions towards their patients over the course of the study period and their subjective reaction towards their patients at the end of the study is largely independent of their initial subjective reaction.

The data presented in this section shows that, while the intensity of the nurse's contacts with a formerly hospitalized mother has little bearing on the patient's post-hospital adjustment, there are significant relationships between a mother's personality and interpersonal functioning and the capacity to profit from nursing intervention.

Turning finally to the question of rehospitalization, what can be said about women who required rehospitalization during the course of the study, as contrasted with women remaining out of the hospital during the period of the study? Looking at our measures of personality and social role adjustment among these 17 rehospitalized mothers, as contrasted with the personality and social adjustment of the 27 mothers remaining out of the hospital, mothers more likely to be rehospitalized were older at the time of the first rehospitalization ($p < .01$), more likely to have had a more chronic adjustment prior to the aftercare study with a longer period of time between onset of symptoms and first hospitalization ($p < .03$) and a larger total number of hospitalizations ($p < .01$); in their capacity for closeness, mothers rehospitalized during the course of the study show greater conflict in their capacity for sustaining such close and satisfying relationships ($p < .01$). Consistent with their conflict in establishing mutuality, in their attitudes towards childcare, when contrasted with mothers remaining out of the hospital during the two year duration of the aftercare study, these rehospitalized mothers express childcare attitudes indicating that they believe, less than mothers remaining out of the hospital, in the desirability of fostering reciprocity or mutuality with the child ($p < .01$) and believe, less than these mothers remaining out of the hospital, that the mother's own needs can be differentiated from those of her child ($p < .001$). Finally, it should be noted that these mothers rehospitalized during the course of the study also report greater life-event stress, (without inclusion of hospitalization for mental illness during the course of the aftercare project) both in their own life ($p < .002$) and that of their husbands ($p < .01$).

These mothers rehospitalized during the course of the study also show greater conflict in one area of social adjustment, that of the maternal role, than is true among women not rehospitalized during the course of the study (p < .02), although no significant differences emerge between the social adjustment of rehospitalized mothers and mothers remaining out of the hospital during the study period with regard to such areas of adult social roles as those of housewife, wife, friend, or daughter in her own parental family.

The picture which emerges of these mothers who are rehospitalized during the study period is that they are a group of already chronically ill women who are unable to sustain meaningful relationships with others, an impairment which may be observed in their attitudes towards the care of their own young children, and which has, as its consequence, serious effects in the mother's ability to provide maternal care for her young children. This composite picture of the personality and social adjustment of the rehospitalized mother is given additional empirical weight as a result of a multivariate analysis which seeks to isolate the best predictors of whether a mother will be rehospitalized. Based on the personality and social adjustment data, the three strongest determinants which emerge in a multiple regression analysis are (1) reported stress in own life (p < .001), (2) the social adjustment factor of adaptation to the maternal role, and (3) the picture thematic measure of capacity for meaningful interpersonal relationships. The multiple correlation between these three indices and rehospitalization of .69 accounts for 48% of the common variance, indicating that knowledge of a woman's capacity for interpersonal closeness, her ability to adjust to the maternal role, and the amount of stress experienced in her own life are reasonably good predictors of the degree of her success in remaining out of the hospital.

CONCLUSION

For the mother of a young child, psychiatric hospitalization is a stressful event, not only for the patient herself, but also for her child, her husband, and for other family members. Hospitalization for mental illness has often meant that the mother must separate from her child, her husband and other family members. Children exposed to such a regime are faced with the confusion and family disorganization which amplifies whatever innate predisposition such children have towards later psychopathology. In a child who may be vulnerable, additional disorganization engendered by family disorganization, multiple mothering, foster care, etc., does not seem to be advantageous. The mother, herself, feeling guilty over her abandonment of her responsibilities as mother and homemaker, finds it difficult to take advantage of hospital resources which are provided for her, and yet she is often unable to manage her life outside the hospital.

Both Doniger (1962), and Rice et al. (1971) report that the physical care provided at home for the children of mentally ill mothers absent from the home is markedly worse than when the mother is at home. In addition, frequent maternal rehospitalizations have a particularly deleterious impact on the mental health of these children. It is particularly important to bear in mind the observation of Rice et al. that parental mental illness of such intensity as to require hospitalization appears to be associated with a decrease in the family's capacity to obtain help.

Such observations suggests the importance for the child and the family of providing not only psychiatric assistance for the mentally ill mother herself, but also for the family as a unit (Sussex, 1963). Indeed, the risk of subsequent disturbance in the child as a result of the crisis of hospitalization, independently or in interaction with genetic factors and transmission of irrationality across the generation, bespeaks the need for effective intervention both for mother herself, as well as for the whole family unit.

REFERENCES

Doniger, C. R. Children whose mothers are in a mental hospital. *Journal of Child Psychology and Psychiatry*, 1962, *3*, 165–173.

Grunebaum, H., Gamer, E., and Cohler, B. The spouse in depressed families. In H. Morrison (Ed.), *Depressed parents and their children*. New York: Grune and Stratton, 1981.

Grunebaum, H., and Weiss, J. Planning for joint admission. In H. Grunebaum, J. Weiss, B. Cohler, D. Gallant, and C. Hartman, *Mentally ill mothers and their children*. Chicago: The University of Chicago Press, 1975, 4–82.

Main, T. Mothers with children in a psychiatric hospital. *Lancet*, 1958, *2*, 845–847.

Rice, E., Ekdahl, M., and Miller, L. *Children of mentally ill parents*. New York: Behavioral Publications, 1971.

Sussex, J. Factors influencing the emotional impact on children of an acutely psychotic mother in the home. In *Southern Medical Journal*, 1963, *56*, 1245–1249.

Van Der Walde, P., Meeks, D., Grunebaum, H., and Weiss, J. Joint admission of mothers and children to a state hospital. *Archives of General Psychiatry*, 1968, *18*, 706–711.

The Preventive Approach
to Children at High Risk
for Psychopathology and Psychosis

E. James Anthony, MD

ABSTRACT. Primary prevention, as applied to the offspring of psychotically-disturbed parents, should be directed not only at the transmission of psychosis to the next generation of adults but also at the relief of suffering and psychopathology in the children, keeping in mind that the two may be causally related and that genetic and environmental factors are constantly interacting. Although one can develop preventive programs from preconceptions of psychotic transmission, and apply them on a trial and error basis, one must bear in mind the presence of interest and acquired resiliences in high-risk subjects and learn from their efforts.

The prospective-longitudinal study of children at high genetic risk for psychosis has not only opened up new ways of examining the complementarity of nature and nurture, together with the "natural history" of psychosis in the making, but it has also made primary prevention much more feasible since one is able to identify vulnerability before it becomes manifest as mental disorder. Since schizophrenia has a greater prevalence and a higher incidence than manic-depression, it has become the main focus for risk research and preventive interventions have been devised and tried out mainly with respect to it. Both these major so-called functional psychoses are no longer regarded as discrete disease entities but increasingly in terms of "spectrum disorders" (Rosenthal et al., 1968).

There are four crucial questions affecting the possibility of preventive interventions:

1. Is the transmission process genetically or environmentally determined or both?

E. James Anthony is Blanche F. Ittleson Professor of Child Psychiatry and Director of the Edison Child Development Research Center, Washington University Medical School, St. Louis, MO.

2. Is the goal the prevention of psychopathology of varying severity that occurs in the offspring of psychotics from infancy onward or is the aim restricted to the prevention of psychosis in the adult?
3. Is the concept and pursuit of prevention itself undesirable or should one strive for the optimal well-being of the individual at risk with non-specific intervention?
4. Should one regard intervention as a one-shot effort or should it be applied continuously or intermittently through the life cycle of the individual?

These questions will be approached in this presentation with schizophrenia in mind but they apply equally to the domain of manic-depression.

The genetic-constitutional theory of schizophrenia is undeniably a primary factor in transmission, although it is still not clear exactly what is transmitted genetically or how it is transmitted. Mehl (1962) has postulated that what is inherited is "a subtle neurointegrative defect" that he termed "schizotaxia." According to him, all schizotaxic individuals develop a "schizotypic" personality organization, but most of these, given favorable interpersonal regimes, remain well-compensated "schizotypes," without signs of mental disease, although they may show some indications of "cognitive slippage and other minimal neurological aberrations." Under conditions of environmental disadvantage, a psychotic change occurs and schizophrenia ensues. This thesis fits in with the view of schizophrenia as a spectrum disorder ranging in the extent of disintegration. Heredity is a *necessary* but not sufficient prerequisite for the development of manifest psychosis, with other factors such as obstetrical complications or environmental stresses being required (Gottesman & Shields, 1972). Fish (1975) has claimed on the basis of an intensive longitudinal observation of infants at genetic risk for schizophrenia that repeated tests have revealed periods of "pan-developmental retardation" in about half of the offspring of schizophrenic mothers, during which time there is a widespread disorganization of maturation, variable profiles of deficits and a fluctuating course of development. Erlenmeyer-Kimling and her colleagues (1977) who are strong protagonists of a genetically-determined diathesis have found early attentional disorders to be present in high-risk children and regard this as an important intermediate variable in the transmission of schizophrenia. If such neurobiological deficits do exist, does it render prevention an impossible dream unresponsive to any environmental attempts at rectification? The proponents of this view deny this, although they tend to consider current intervention projects as premature and unlikely to succeed because of insufficient etiological knowledge. Nevertheless, they do not exclude prevention as a future prospect based on the modification of such intermediary deficits as attentional disturbances. There is an "iffiness" in such pronouncements: If transmission is genetically based, and if there are intervening neuropsychological deficits as evidence of this, and if such deficits can be correctable, *then* the manifestation of psychosis would be prevented; but, the transmission into subsequent generations would proceed unabated.

The environmentalists, on the other hand, are not only, understandably, more optimistic in their approach but are presently engaged in interventions, often proclaiming defiantly that they are not prepared to wait for a total knowledge of transmission before intervening. They tend to pay lip service to the genetic hypothesis but do not take it so seriously that it hampers their preventive efforts. There may be an unalterable substratum to psychosis that is physically based, but for them, the environmental factors are so predominant that the lot of the individual can be, according to them, significantly improved by altering the interactional, communicative and learning milieu of psychosis. Bleuler (1978) has amassed the data on both genetic and environmental sides and has seriously questioned whether environment can make schizophrenia. (Some environmental theorists have suggested the transmission of psychological factors through the child-rearing process with each generation adding its quota of psycho-genetically-induced vulnerability so that schizophrenia emerges after increasingly bad upbringing over many generations. There is, of course, no hard evidence for this.) What Bleuler has questioned is whether one can "learn irrationality" at the knees of one's parents. He does not doubt that the schizophrenic milieu generated by a psychotic parent can cause a great deal of suffering and unhappiness (in addition to a great deal of courage and compassion), but suffering is not schizophrenia. He has no question that gene-environment interaction does occur as part of the "natural history" of schizophrenia, but he is clearly not prepared, at this time, to disentangle cause from effect. What impresses him with regard to high-risk children is not that a small number (barely 10 percent) develop schizophrenia and that others suffer from the parental illness, but that an appreciable number of them show an extraordinary resilience to the impingements of psychosis. Garmezy (1971) and Anthony (1978) believe that more attention should be paid to these resilient children who "love well, work well, play well and expect well" although immersed from infancy in the "subculture of psychosis." Both Garmezy and Anthony have suggested that the proper study of such "superphrenic" children may eventually furnish us with the critical answers to problems of prevention since they have to prevent a disorder in themselves by their own acquisition of competences and coping skills.

Anthony (1974) has put forward the view that certain specific cognitive and affective dissonances, especially in the mother, may be assimilated by children during their development and that the way they feel, think and construct the world around them, in Piaget's terms, may be acquired by subtle processes of internalization. If such was the case, it might be possible to unlearn such incongruities and learn more congruous ones. To this end, he has constructed the risk-vulnerability model and applied it directly to a prevention program.

Within this model, the first task for the interventionist is to separate children of high risk and high vulnerability, that is, those who have been exposed to specific and non-specific psychotic stresses and those who from early infancy have displayed a testable high level of vulnerability. He has devised a battery of tests by which such hypersensitive individuals can be distinguished. The model includes the reduction or neutralization of risk factors, the stimulation of parents and others to foster competences, the helping of children to improve their own cognitive and social skills, the attenuation of stressor experiences, and the organization of comprehensive support systems. Anthony has been impressed by the "representational competence" shown by some of the "invulnerables," meaning by this, their capacity to construct a frame of reference that makes the psychotic experience meaningful and therefore manageable. He has commented on the dispassionate clinical way in which many of these children view the parental illness and distance themselves from too close an involvement with it. If such survival strategies can be "naturally" acquired by these children, it may be, according to him, possible to teach them to the less resilient offspring. In these interventions, he made a comparison of compensatory, corrective, classical and cathartic interventions which involve working with the high-risk children to counterbalance unfavorable environmental circumstances, to correct "mystifications" with regard to the manifestations of psychosis, to abreact the feelings of fear, shame, guilt, anger and resentment that pervade their lives and to use simple "child guidance" types of psychotherapy individually or in groups, as modes of prevention. All of them had short term ameliorations and he suggested that a better test of the efficacy of the program would be to continue it intermittently throughout the period of development.

Experience has led to the conclusion that an epigenetic view of psychosis is the most helpful one to have in mind with regard to prevention since it may limit one's expectations while still encouraging us to proceed with our interventions. Prevention might not be total, but any amount of prevention would be worthwhile. What one wants to prevent is clearly not only long-term psychosis in the adult but also the wide admixture of psychopathology that one encounters in the off-spring of these children, some of which are reactive while others are antecedents to adult psychosis. Bower (1972) feels that prevention and promotion of mental health have been too tightly tied to mental illness and that one should be as concerned with the many other endpoints in human failure. He feels that preventive and promotion programs need to be anchored to adverse conditions in all their manifestations. He would like to establish an integrative institution in which health, family, play, and school form a compact and com-pelling children's ecological unit in which weaknesses and strengths in one area can be related to weaknesses and strengths in others so that helpful synergies can be cultivated. This type of unit could form the basis for more specific attempts at prevention. Whatever one does should be against the background of the total development of the child and adolescent, since there is now good evidence that *one* dose of prevention can do very little against the *continued* encroachments of subtle and gross pathological onslaughts on the child. I can do no better, in terms of hopefulness, than to quote Bleuler (1978) when he says:

> Long-term upbringing by two schizophrenic parents does not foredoom a child to be schizophrenic or even abnormal. . . Normal development can take place in the face of total neglect, copious "teaching of irrationality" and the total degeneration of the imaginative world of the parents. . . Despite the miserable childhoods, and despite the presumably tainted genes, most off-spring of schizophrenics manage to lead normal productive lives. Indeed, after studying a number of family histories, one is left with the impression that pain and suffering can have a steeling, a hardening effect on some children, rendering them capable of mastering life with all its obstacles.

If one can be as optimistic about the self-preventive capacities that can develop as a response to adversity, surely one can be hopeful about intervention programs closely modelled on such self-generated preventions.

We should keep in mind in our preventive work the new understanding accruing from our careful, longitudinal studies that can also tell us how our interventions are working. What we need is close, continuous and intensive contact with subjects in sufficient numbers and ranging over all types of psychosis so that generalizations regarding primary prevention become feasible and applicable. To work successfully with prevention, as with therapy, one must cultivate an enduring preventive alliance, an unobtrusive monitoring of everyday life, prevention based on self-preventive measures, and a reasonably optimistic outlook. The program must be aimed not only at the prevention of long-term adult disorders but even more importantly, at the diminition of childhood suffering and psychopathology. If the later effort is causally beneficial to the former, so much the better. The child may be father to the man even in the field of prevention.

REFERENCES

Anthony, E. J. *Children at psychiatric risk*. E. J. Anthony and C. Chiland (Eds.), New York: John Wiley, 1974.

Anthony, E. J., C. Koupernik, and C. Chiland (Eds.). *The child in his family: Vulnerable children*, 1978, *4*, New York: John Wiley.

Bleuler, M. *The schizophrenic disorders: Long-term patients and family studies*. Translated by S. Clemens. New Haven: Yale University Press, 1978.

Bower, E. M. KISS and kids: A mandate for prevention. In *American Journal of Orthopsychiatry*, 1972, *42* 4, 556–565.

Fish, B. Biologic antecedents of psychosis in children. In *The Biology of the Major Psychoses*. D. X. Freedman (Ed.), New York: Raven Press, 49–80, 1975.

Garmezy, N. Vulnerability research and the issue of primary prevention. In *American Journal of Orthopsychiatry*, 1971, *41* 1, 101–116.

Gottesman, I., and Shields, J. *Schizophrenia and genetics*. New York: Academic Press, 1972.

Mehl, P. E. Schizotaxia, schizotypy, schizophrenia. In *American Psychologist*, 1962, *17*, 827–838.

Rosenthal, D., and Kety, S. (Eds.) *The transmission of schizophrenia*. New York: Pergamon Press, 1968.

Rutschmann, J., Cornblatt, B., and Erlenmeyer-Kimling, L. Sustained attention in children at risk for schizophrenia. In *Archive of General Psychiatry*, 1977, *34*, 571–575.

THE INCARCERATED PARENT

The Offender as Parent

Judith F. Weintraub

ABSTRACT. It is to the benefit of the offender, the children, the prison and society as a whole to recognize and deal with the special needs of families of offenders so as to maintain the family as a functioning unit. Commission of a crime does not necessarily bear any connection to a person's ability as a parent. The helping profession must deal with the needs and best interests of the children with whom they are working and maintain contact with the imprisoned parent, notwithstanding the social stigma involved.

The 1960s saw a revolution in the recognition of the rights of large segments of our society heretofore neatly labelled, packaged and hidden away out of sight, their needs unrecognized and untended. One of the groups brought—almost literally—out of the dungeon and into the light of day in this process were the inmates of the prisons. Before the period of the late 60s and early 70s, prison inmates were almost unknown to the ordinary social welfare organizations, their needs being addressed by the handful of prisoner aid organizations in existence around the country, some of which traced their origins back to the social revolution of the early 19th century. If the general public thought about prisoners at all, it was generally in the stereotype of George Raft and Jimmy Cagney—psychopaths who, if they had a wife, was generally the dyed brass blond gum chewing "moll." Children were never in evidence. There was no hint that the person serving a sentence in a prison could be anything other than a career criminal and cer-

Judith F. Weintraub is a Criminal Justice Consultant, 15 Washington Place, New York, NY 10003.

tainly no reference to a life which could be recognized as normal by anyone in the society.

When the "revolt of the powerless" of the 1960s followed the draft resisters, middle-class marijuana users, and Black and Hispanics into the prison, prisoners lost their anonoymous label of convict and began to emerge as people, individuals with real needs, some of which should be met because it was their right to have them met, some of which should be met because of humanitarian grounds, some of which would benefit the orderly running of the prisons, some of which would improve the safety of society and some of which could have—might have—an important positive effect on the next generation, their children.

Those who consider themselves "hard-headed realists" tend to dismiss the first two reasons as being the misguided efforts of "bleeding-heart do gooders." Prison administrators, however, know the disruptive effect which serious unmet family problems can have on the functioning of an inmate and studies have demonstrated that parolees with a family to return to commit far fewer violations of their parole than do those who return to nothing. (For a discussion of the published studies, see Eva Lee Homer, "Inmate-Family Ties: Desirable but Difficult," Federal Probation, Vol. 43, No. 1, March 1979, p. 47.) Experience is clear on the desirable effect on children of maintaining a functioning family unit.

As of January, 1981, there were 320,000 people in State and Federal prisons in this country, and the figure is rising. Probably no one has determined how many of these prisoners have children with whom they are in close contact, but any prison officer who has ever been on duty in a visiting room will attest to the fact that there are many.

Over the last ten years, there have been many surface changes which recognize the needs of a prisoner as family member and parent. In my State, New York, a bus system was established to provide free transportation to the prisons for families of prisoners. Visiting rooms were changed drastically. The wire mesh screens which divided the long tables in the visiting room, with inmates sitting on one side and families on another, have long since come down. (One mother tried to explain the presence of the screen through which her young daughter had kissed her father as a filter for germs. With today's television sophisticated youth, that explanation did not hold.) The table has been replaced in many cases by small groupings of chairs where a family can sit together and talk in some semblance of privacy. Some prisons have provided toys and books for the children while they are waiting. In some prison towns, volunteers, often church connected, have established reception centers where the families can freshen up after what is usually a long bus ride. (Large prisons are not generally placed close to the large urban centers from which a majority of their inmates, and hence the inmates' families, come.) These changes have made it easier for families to visit and perhaps have resulted in more families making such visits. The placement of telephones in prisons which are available for use by prisoners (with tight limitations on the place to which the call can be made, the number of calls, and the length of time of each conversation) has facilitated rapid communication with family members. But there are a series of problems which these surface changes do not touch, problems which highlight the basic impotence and frustration of a prisoner's life, problems which affect the maintenance of a family unit or at least the maintenance of the prisoner within the family unit and which ultimately affect the orderly operation of the prison and the safety of society itself.

If the prisoner's family has no phone, he cannot call them. If they do not visit, he cannot talk to them. If they have moved since his arrest, he cannot write to them. If they do not write to him, he does not know what is going on. If one or both parties cannot write, a reality in many cases, correspondence becomes meaningless anyway. And if there is a family problem, the prisoner has no way of finding out what is going on. Prisons are not structured with community-based field offices which can find out what has happened to the inmate's wife who was seven months pregnant when he was sentenced and has not been heard from since. There are few local organizations which even deal with the problems of inmates, much less have the resources to be able to provide that type of local information gathering.

From the family's point of view, there are a myriad of problems caused by the imprisonment of a parent with which they get little help. In addition to the essentials of food, shelter and clothing, frequently paid for by welfare, others are the internal reactions of shame, loss, guilt, and rejection being experienced by the wife and children, feelings often intensified by the social service agencies with which they come into contact. Present particularly when the family member has gone to prison for the first time, there is the bewildering new world to understand in order to maintain contact. (For a more detailed description of the stresses on the family of a prisoner, see Schwartz and Weintraub, "The Prisoner's Wife: A Study in Crisis," *Federal Probation*, Vol. 38, No. 4, December 1974, p. 20, and Weintraub, "The

Delivery of Services to Families of Prisoners,'' *Federal Probation*, Vol 40, No. 4, December 1976, p. 28). There have been isolated attempts around the country to deal with these problems, which are described in another article in this journal which is authored by the Executive Director of one excellent such program located in Hartford, Connecticut.

But the answer does not lie in creating more, specialized programs, particularly in a period of severe financial retrenchment. The message needs to be heard by all of the human services practitioners who come into contact with families of prisoners in the course of their regular work.

First and foremost, it must be recognized that *there is no connection between criminality and parenting*. If it is a given fact that it is preferable to maintain a complete family unit whenever possible, then it follows that the parents should be evaluated on their performance as parents, and not on outside factors. The factors that cause or contribute to an individual's criminality may also affect his functioning as a parent. Someone whose violent criminal behavior traces its roots back to an abused childhood is likely to be an abusing parent. But the response and the intervention should be based on that fact and not on the criminal actions.

Workers in the helping professions, who are not supposed to pass moral value judgements on their clients, freqently show a strong negative reaction to hearing that one of the parents is in prison, a reaction which may be carried over to the family itself. We are conditioned to abhor criminals. This casting out of society of those who break its laws is one of the ways which society has of making sure that the rest of us will obey those laws.

The problem, of course, is that individuals are not sent out of the reach of their families and that their period of exile is only a temporary one. They will be returning. The family must cope with their continued existence. The children must adapt to existence, absence and return. The prisoner needs a family to return to.

In addition to the lack of recognition, support and assistance from the helping professions with these problems, families also have to deal with the negative bias against their situation.

This negative bias can take many different guises. I was once told by someone who held an important position in the criminal justice/corrections hierarchy in New York State that he though it might be a mistake to encourage prisoners to stay with their families because, after all, it was the demands of the wives which caused so much of the criminality in the first place. Such a person is not likely to foster programs which will make it easier for an inmate to maintain contact with wife and children.

There is the belief, embodied in law in many states, that conviction for a felony is sufficient evidence to warrant termination of parental rights. There are laws which deny a prisoner any say in adoption proceedings for his own children. In some cases, the prisoner/parent does not even have to be notified.

The problem becomes particularly noticeable when the children have had to be placed in foster care as a result of the parent's imprisonment. Anyone who has worked with prisoners' families has had the experience of trying to convince workers in the foster care system that children should be allowed and even encouraged to visit their parents in prison. What is almost a conspiracy of silence develops around the missing parent, denying the child the support needed to come through difficult times and almost guaranteeing that future problems will be intensified. Children have a compelling need to know their parents. It is common for adults to search for their parents they never knew, or one whom they "lost" in their youth. How much better for all concerned if the tie were maintained unbroken.

Along with the bias of many in the helping professions against prisoners is the ignorance of the special problems posed by having a family member in jail. If a parent has died, social workers, psychologists, and psychiatrists know how to deal with the effect on the child. If a parent has been removed for a long period of time for military service or in a job overseas, the problems for the children are recognized. There is not always realization that many of these problems are shared by children of inmates complicated by the accompanying shame and secrecy associated with jail.

The inclusion of incarcerated parents in this journal is a sign that the profession is beginning to realize the special status of their children. The reasons for doing so rest on our own best interests. If the family unit is the building block of our society, then a healthy community requires families that are intact and functioning. If children are our future, then it is to our own benefit to help them develop in the best way possible.

"My Daddy's Number is C-92760"

James E. Hughes, M.Div, MS, PhD

ABSTRACT. Inmates in a maximum security prison, trained in college credit Pedology courses and referred to as Play Monitors, supervised a play area in the prison visiting room and provided the framework where children could play in a safe and structured way with materials appropriate to their developmental needs. The availability and strength of the Play Monitors ego enabled the child's ego to master, in age appropriate ways, the circumstances of the visiting room rather than being lost in fantasy or random motoric behavior. Thus, children and parents could function in a more normal manner promoting the mental health development of the family unit.

"These people must live like pigs, look at all the trash they left around where they were sitting."

"They don't care about their kids, they let them run wild and bother other people visiting."

"These aren't fit parents, look at them yelling and hitting at their kids all the time."

These are comments made by adults about the behavior of adults and children in a prison visiting room which does not provide adequate facilities to meet the needs of children and their parents. Just as it is not possible to remove the human eye and discuss its function separate from the body, neither, is it possible to understand the meaning of the prison visit without having an understanding of the "prison experience." If a prison permits five three-hour visits a month, seven hundred and twenty hours remain for an inmate to "serve time," "do time," or "pull time."

There is no higher or more impenetrable wall than the reality of distrust that overwhelms the fabric of all prison experience. There is an ever present, all pervasive feeling that no one is to be trusted—no one. The fear is that whatever is said to another person, friend, foe or even in confidence to a counselor, chaplain or mental health pro-

James E. Hughes is Professor of Pedology at the Community College of Allegheny County, Inc., Pittsburgh, PA and is Past Chairperson of the Board of the Pittsburgh Psychoanalytic Center, Inc.

79

fessional, will find its way back into the "jacket" or file of the inmate and be used against him at some future hearing. This mistrust is compounded by the fact that prisons depend on inmate informers supplying information about other inmates. To act as a "snitch" or an informer is a way for inmates to gain favor in the eyes of the prison administration. Frequently "snitches" or informers "set up" other inmates by leaving contraband in a cell and then surreptitiously reporting it to the prison administration. When the planted contraband is found, usually money, drugs or drug paraphernalia, the "set up" or innocent inmate is punished and this infraction of the rules will go into the permanent record, affecting the future possibility of release. Prisons use informers because they feel it is a necessary way to control the security of the institution. Perhaps the savage rage directed against alleged informers in the New Mexico prison riot illustrates the fear and hatred of the system as investigated by *Time* magazine (1980).

Along with the basic mistrust of human relationships is the cessation of normal heterosexual relationships. Thomas (1972) reports that homosexual acting out and self-inflicted wounds reflect this severe deprivation. In prison language, "Mind your ass or someone else will" is a way of saying, "Be on your guard, don't get yourself in situations where you'll get raped." To illustrate this comment, an inmate deliberately brushed against a newly-arrived inmate who was small of stature with blond hair and blue eyes. Although the new inmate was not at all at fault, he apologized but soon realized that he was being set up to see if he would be a "pushover" and thus a candidate for intimidation and rape. Although the newly-arrived inmate had never been in a state prison before, his county jail time, awaiting post conviction motions, had opened his eyes. He turned and started a fight, deliberately choosing to get into trouble, rather than be one of the "sissies" chased around the yard by other inmates.

Within the inmate populations there are hierarchies of power where rival gangs with paramilitary ranks and duties struggle for control of the system. Intimidations, beatings, stabbings, murders and various other acts are common forms of behavior between the groups.

There is no fundamental privacy when inmates void and defecate in a crowded cell or when toilets are flushed en masse only at specific times. The author has never seen a toilet lid in any prison, including the most modern. Rather, one sees the unitized stainless steel wash basin toilet combination, without a toilet lid. The concern is toilet lids can be used as weapons, inflict self-injury or make disruptive noise similar to rubbing a cup against cell bars.

The quality of food varies in prisons but the ever present steam table changes the taste of food into a bland sameness with a loss of vital nutrients. The author has never seen a chair in a prison mess hall, one that has four legs and a back that can be moved up to a table at a comfortable distance for the eater. Rather one sees benches or stools made of hardwood or cold steel bolted to the floor. The concern is that chairs not bolted down and with a back can be picked up and used as weapons in combat.

Life in prison slows down as if in slow motion. "Street action," that is, people moving freely about anywhere in any direction, at any speed, vehicular traffic moving at different rates of speed, the motion of quick step and go—is absent. One inmate released after 13 years in prison found himself to be exceedingly anxious at street intersections.

Within this highly volatile, never-ending climate of despair and dread, a prison visit can be an extremely important event. The author (1974), having spent a decade teaching and working on a research project within prison systems, has never met an inmate who is "laid back" or indifferent about the possibility of being released—including those sentenced to death. A visitor, particularly a loved person, represents a handle on reality, someone not part of the system, someone who can be trusted and work in behalf of the inmate's efforts for release.

The visiting procedure for inmates and their visitors is usually complex and always filled with tension. The prison administration does not have the same kind of control over visitors as it does with the inmates inside the cell blocks. The concern is that contraband, usually drugs, but also weapons will be passed to the inmate or acts of violence will occur.

In Pennsylvania State Correctional Institutions, each civilian visitor must fill out a questionnaire and be placed on the institution's approved visiting list before being permitted to visit a resident. Inmates are permitted five visits a month from 8:30 a.m. to 8:00 p.m. daily including holidays. No more than four adults are permitted per visit, but there is no stated policy concerning the number of children who may visit a resident. The visiting time may be extended to a maximum of three hours if the visiting room is not crowded but only one hour on weekends and holidays.

As Schwartz and Weintraub (1974) report, prison systems were not designed to meet such family needs as visiting. Prisons are usually located in remote areas which means that visitors and children have an ordeal of travel before they arrive at the prison and begin the ordeal of step one in the visiting procedure.

Most prison visiting rooms were not originally designed or used for the purpose of visiting. The space that was used when a prisoner received a twenty-minute visit once a month, does not accommodate the number of people who are permitted to come five times a month, for a three-hour visit. The visiting rooms used today may be filled with booths where people talk over a phone and look at each other through a plexiglass window. They may sit across a table with a barrier attached to the underneath of the table with a screen on top that people can talk through. Some prisons permit "contact" visiting where people are permitted to sit by each other without a barrier.

Within the framework of a prison visit, adult needs, as previously described, are urgent and often take priority over the needs of the visiting children. These needs may be expressed in the following manner, "What did you find out, how is my appeal going?" "Did you tell the lawyer what I said?" "We've got to get more money for the lawyer if I'm ever going to get out of here." "How much money can you leave for me today?" "Why didn't you write to me last month?" It is quite possible that somewhere in the visiting room is a sign that reads: "ROWDY CHILDREN WILL BE THE CAUSE OF YOUR VISIT TO BE TERMINATED." Therefore, adults are under pressure to keep the children quiet and still—but what young child, after a long trip to the prison, in the presence of a parent who is not the "at home" parent, can be made to sit still for three hours? What usually happens is the child is excluded from the adult relationships in the sense that the "at home" parent is less available to the child because of the nature of the involvement with the inmate parent. When there is no provision in the visiting room to promote age appropriate goal directed behavior, the children place demands on both parents often prompting them to respond with verbal threats or physical punishment such as, "Stop that running around or they'll keep you here." "Be quiet or I'll take my belt off." "Stop crying or I'll really smack you." One may also see vigorous shaking, slapping, spanking, or pinching of children to stop their misbehavior.

In response, the children, correctly perceiving these parental actions as aggression directed against them, respond by intruding aggressively into the visits of other people, pushing chairs, fighting or running and chasing after other children, yanking on the vending machine knobs, or coping with uncertainty by withdrawing into sleep. When the visit is finally over, these childrens' conflicts are not resolved and they leave more exhausted and more conflict ridden than at the beginning of the visit.

There is a way for adults and children to have a meaningful experience during a prison visit and that is when an area, designated for children within the visiting room, can be provided with adequate supervision. The author, by securing a small grant, was able to change the visiting room experience of a maximum security prison, by providing a small play area within the visiting room. This area was equipped with child size tables and chairs as well as appropriate play materials and supervised by inmates who were enrolled in college credit child development courses in the prison education program.

In the fall of 1972, inmates and correctional staff responded to a questionnaire designed by inmates to determine whether or not the visiting room should be altered to include a supervised area for children. The overwhelming response was in the affirmative.

Next, the first year of a two-year child development curriculum from the Community College of Allegheny County, Pittsburgh, Pennsylvania, was taught to inmates leading to an Associate Science Degree in Pedology (the study of the growing child). The curriculum reflected a dynamic understanding of childhood and thus it was important to discuss developmental issues of various ages, and ways adults could be supportive of children within the structure of a prison visit. For example, a four-year-old who has made gains in developing a separate sense of self within the framework of Mahler's (1968) separation individuation process, may regress as a way to cope with an unfamiliar environment, such as a prison visit, by sucking on a crayon. Before removing the crayon from the child's mouth, the educational focus was on assessing the child's behavior and then encouraging and supporting the child's creative expression with the crayon, while maintaining the goal of facilitating the use of words as a way to express feelings.

After one year of planning and teaching the first year of a child development curriculum, the play area opened on November 27, 1973, at 9:00 a.m. At the same time, the author secured a grant to provide a recreational room for the correctional staff including wall to wall carpet, air conditioning, comfortable chairs and tables, and a ping-pong table. Thus, both inmates and correctional staff were provided with new and helpful additions that recognized the legitimate needs of both.

When the play area opened, the children, rather than engaging in run and chase games, had a place where they could express their needs in a developmentally appropriate manner, supervised by an inmate trained in child development.

For example, two year olds enjoyed filling and emptying the sorter boxes, reflecting their interest in containment and release. Three year olds in parallel play explored the function of play objects such as the snap blocks and used them adaptively in their play. Four year olds in cooperative play created home experiences of preparing and serving meals to children who were assigned various family roles. Five year olds used the family hand puppets to reflect social relationships as well as to sublimate aggressive and frightening feelings. School-age children used materials where cognitive mastery reflected growing skills and accomplishments.

One form of play was for the child to re-create a comfortable kind of reality from home as if to remind him the world outside the prison still existed. For example, many children used the play dishes to recreate the daily familiar experience of eating at home. By bringing a familiar life experience into the unfamiliar, children could begin to work on the meaning of the visiting experience rather than evading it through random motoric behavior or passive withdrawal. Feeling comfortable in the unfamiliar, children began to ask questions concerning the prison, such as "Why was the guard killed?" "Are children beaten here?" and to feel less anxious knowing that the violence of the institution would not turn against them.

Children also used play defensively as a way to blot out anxiety producing perceptions. When adults were involved in conversations or other activities that did not include children, they concentrated on play as if the adult exclusion did not exist. For example, puzzle play imposed structure on the fragmenting experience of being excluded from parental involvement, thus lessening potential trauma.

Due to the design of the author's play area project, children and parents had free access with each other. Children could take their play interests (drawing a picture), back to where their parents were sitting and parents were free to be actively involved with their children in the play area. This interaction enhanced an inmate's sense of parent-hood. Some inmate parents were now a captive to their child's interests and could no longer evade parental responsibilities as in the past, by being absent from the home and having little parental responsibility for their child.

A five year old came into the supervised play area wearing a tee shirt with his father's institutional number printed on the front. He said in a proud manner, "C-92760 is my daddy's number." Through the interaction of this child and with his father in the play area, the child is saying he knows his father, his father exists, his father is a real person, which is essential for a child to feel when a parent is absent from much of the child's life. For the inmate parent, there is the concrete realization that there is a family to come home to, which enhances a growing sense of family solidarity and responsibility.

When an inmate parent is deprived of a sustained relationship with the family, this affects the inmate parent's personality development, as well as the personality development of the children. Following Mahler's (1968) research, a child's integrated sense of self evolves from his capacity to develop an integrated view of the "good" but also "bad" or frustrating parents. In the imprisoned parent, children see a parent who is considered "bad." There is very little an imprisoned parent can do that communicates to the child the "good" parent. The day the parent is taken to prison, that parent becomes a person society calls "bad." Due to the restrictions in many institutions, the role of the parent in the visiting room is a passive one. They cannot purchase foodstuffs or drink for their spouse and children because they are not permitted to have money. The "at home" parent has to bring money in order to purchase foodstuffs, drink, cigarettes or photographs. The inmate parent cannot offer a gift or receive a gift from the spouse or children in the visiting room. The inmate parent is not permitted to take their child to the bathroom because it may be located behind a set of locked gates which is off limits. Nor may the inmate parent be permitted to take his child to get a drink because the fountain is located outside of the visiting room. Consequently, the child does not have the experience of the "good" parent being a provider even in the place where the parent lives.

Being deprived of the "good" parent affects the child's capacity to develop an integrated sense of the good and bad self essential for healthy growth and development. Children who do not succeed in establishing true object constancy by building up enduring representations of the good but also bad parent, cannot achieve lasting identification with their parent or potential parental figures. When the ego is not able to integrate a cohesive sense of self through stable parental figures, adult and adolescent acting out behavior is possible.

During a child development class discussion, an inmate student recalled the childhood experience of visiting his father in prison. Although at an early age he was aware that his father was in prison, he was repeatedly told he was visiting his father's place of work. After the father was released and living in the same neighborhood, the inmate remembered calling him a "jailbird." Years later the son, now an adult, is an inmate in the same maximum security prison and today others may refer to him as a "jailbird."

In recent years, spaces designated for visiting children have been developed which have caused additional problems for children and parents. These are areas that do not permit children and parents to have free access with each other. In one prison, a large fenced in yard was provided next to a designated children's room that was separate from the visiting room. Parents were not permitted to be in either space. The children did not have free access to their parents. To separate parents from children in this manner creates additional levels of separation and confusion. Further, when assigned inmates, due to lack of understanding the real developmental issues, twirl children around and make them sit in a circle repeating the alphabet, it only increases the strain and stress that the children are already feeling.

There are prisons that permit parents to keep their young children with them. The author has visited Holloway prison in London, the woman's prison in Frankfort, Germany, and one outside of Bern, Switzerland. A mental health consultant (Personal Communications, 1974) to the Frankfort prison reported high incidences of feeding disturbances among the children who live with their mothers in that prison. Escalona (1940) observed in a women's prison in Boston, where mothers could keep their young children, that children's feeding disturbances were related to the tense atmosphere of prison life. It is the author's opinion that before children are permitted to live with parents in prison, extensive research be conducted.

In establishing a supervised play area for children in prison, many problems must be solved. Inmates may tire of the work for it is demanding and exhausting working with children in the stressful situation of a prison. Prison life can quickly grind down an inmate's enthusiasm and commitment. Some inmates leave the project for they feel that the prison administration does not recognize their work with children, for they are continually turned down for a better classification. If the visiting procedure is under a new security directive where all inmates must be stripped searched, with examination of genital and anal areas, some inmates may decline to participate further in the children's work because of their dislike for this procedure. Conflicts do develop between correctional officers and assigned inmates. For example, an officer may feel an inmate is becoming too familiar with the adults in the visiting room or should not be permitted to eat in the children's area, or have only one inmate working at a time even when the space is crowded with children. However, maintaining a well planned supervised play area provides a unique experience which enhances the healthy development for each family member—the child, inmate parent and the "at home" parent.

Because of the difficulties involved in prison visiting, it is understandable that sustained visiting takes a lot of patience and endurance on everyone's part. For those families who can maintain consistent visiting, trusted and valued relationships can persist so that upon release there is less chance of the "ex-offender" getting back into trouble.

A significant number of the readers of this journal are teachers who by the nature of their profession are aware of the significant developmental issues children might encounter with a parent in prison. For example, teachers know that it is not possible to deal with cognitive achievement without also dealing with emotional development. These important issues are also encountered in a play area in a prison visiting room. The supervising inmate in a play area, similar to a teacher who is understanding of a child's struggles, can support the child's growing self-esteem and the feeling that adults do care about them and their development, which enhances the healthy development of each member of the family.

REFERENCES

Escalona, Sibylle K. Feeding disturbances in very young children. *American Journal of Orthopsychiatry*, 1945, *15*, 76–80.

Thomas, Herbert E. *Regressive behavior in maximum security prisoners (a preliminary communication)*. Presented at the meeting of the American Association for the Advancement of Science, December, 1972.

Hughes, James E. *Play of children in a visiting room of a maximum security prison (a comparison of behavior before play materials were available and after a play situation was provided)*. Doctoral Dissertation, University of Pittsburgh. Ann Arbor, Michigan: University Microfilms, 1974, No. 75-13, 193.

Mahler, Margaret S. On human symbiosis and the vicissitudes of individuation. *Infantile Psychosis*. New York: International Universities Press, Inc., 1968, Vol. I.

Schwartz, Mary C., and Weintraub, Judith F. The prisoner's wife: A study in crisis. *Federal Probation, 1974, 38*(4), 23.

Time magazine, *115*(7), 30-31. February 18, 1980.

The Impact of Incarceration on Children of Offenders

Susan Hoffman Fishman

ABSTRACT. Hundreds of thousands of children experience emotional turmoil each year as the result of the incarceration of a parent. In addition to coping with feelings of grief, anger and rejection, they must deal with the stigma associated with having a relative in prison. Although this article concentrates on the impact of incarceration on both the children of male and female inmates, it also describes the problems encountered by other family members within the family unit. Despite a newfound interest in research and information on children of offenders, there is still a tremendous need for positive and innovative programs that address the problems of this special population.

Jennifer is an 8-year-old, whose father was incarcerated in a Connecticut prison for a felony offense. Her mother brought her to Women in Crisis, a private agency in Hartford, Connecticut, that provides assistance to families of offenders, when she became alarmed at the child's behavior. Jennifer wasn't sleeping well at night and was having nightmares. She was withdrawn and frightened. In response to questions posed by a psychologist where she was asked to complete the following sentences, Jennifer replied, "Mother.....doesn't care." "Father..... doesn't care."

Hundreds of thousands of children like Jennifer experience emotional and physical turmoil each year as a result of the incarceration of a parent. Although there are no national statistics documenting the exact numbers of children affected, estimates can be derived from sample inmate populations. A recent survey in Waterbury, Connecticut showed that amongst a sample of 123 women with male relatives sentenced to Connecticut State correctional institutions, 205 children were left at home. A similar survey in England (Morris, 1965) recorded

Susan Hoffman Fishman is Executive Director, Women in Crisis, Hartford, CT

89

that 415 persons in prison there had documented 928 dependent children. In 1978, 465,778 men and women were incarcerated in state, federal and county institutions (Bureau of Justice Statistics, 1979). If we use the survey samples as a rough indication of the proportion of children residing in families with incarcerated parents, then there were approximately 900,000 children in the United States during 1978 who were forced to cope with dramatic changes in their life situations. In addition to losing friends and self-esteem and experiencing feelings of grief, anger and rejection, they had to deal with the stigma associated with having a relative in prison as well as the turmoil it caused within the family unit.

Even though incarceration impacts children and other family members in increasing numbers and dramatic proportions, historically, relatively little attention has been given to the problem either by social service practitioners (Weintraub, 1976) or through research efforts. Moreover, within the field of corrections itself, which is most directly involved with the problems of inmates and their families, the topic area has not been seriously studied either in literature, through program efforts or as a result of legislative action (Schwartz & Weintraub, 1974). The majority of existing articles have been written since 1972 (Fishman & Cassin, 1981). Although they tend to document the effects of imprisonment on spouses or other adult relatives, few have attempted a thorough examination on the special problems experienced by children of offenders (Sack et al., 1976). A study conducted by Holt and Miller in 1972 seems to have prompted a recent newfound interest in families with loved ones in prison. Using a sample of 412 prisoners incarcerated in a minimum security prison in California, Holt and Miller concluded that inmates who maintained family ties during incarceration were more likely to avoid difficulties and remain out of prison after their initial release. The study has been heavily emphasized by authors and social service providers as a rationale for assisting families of offenders in coping with their own problems so that they can serve as a source of support to the inmate in prison (Adams & Fisher, 1976; Cobean & Power, 1978; Homer, 1979; Fishman & Alissi, 1979). Such support provided to families of offenders may not only benefit the men and women directly involved, but the general society as well.

Although this article will concentrate on the effects of incarceration on children of offenders, it is impossible to understand the subject without also examining the problems encountered by other family members left at home. Morris (1967), in her article on children of male offenders in England, cited two basic factors which determine the extent to which a child suffers from a parent's incarceration: (1) the type of father/child relationship existing before imprisonment, and (2) the effect of separation on the mother (or caretaker) with whom the child lives.

Since only 4–7% of the national inmate population is female, most children of offenders are living with mothers and other female relatives of male offenders. Although some of the problems experienced by children whose mothers are in prison are similar to those encountered by children with fathers in prison, there are some very specific issues relevant only to children of women offenders. For this reason, we will deal separately with the impact of incarceration on spouses and children of male as opposed to female offenders.

IMPACT OF INCARCERATION ON CHILDREN/FAMILIES OF MALE OFFENDERS

Although the entire period of incarceration and subsequent separation is difficult, very specific crisis points have been identified as especially bewildering for the family left at home (Weintraub, 1976; Fishman & Alisssi, 1979). The crisis times include: (1) arrest and pre-trial, (2) sentencing day, (3) initial incarceration, (4) pre/post release, and they correspond with the process which the inmate must follow as he proceeds through the criminal justice system.

Arrest and Pre-Trial

The first crisis occurs for the family when the accused offender is arrested and physically separated from his home. Since arrest is usually sudden and unexpected, family members experience confusion, shock and stress. They often do not believe that the accused could be guilty (Cobean & Power, 1978) and rarely understand the complex court process which is suddenly set in motion. Family members whose loved ones remain incarcerated before trial because they cannot raise the money for bail are plunged into a situation where they must quickly learn legal terminology and resources available, and, they must withstand constant pressures and demands from the inmate who wants desperately to get out of jail. In many instances, family members without financial resources for bail are burdened with a constant sense of guilt and frustration. Because the pre-trial court process can extend from several months to a year or more, families are unable to plan concretely for their future and maintain themselves in a state of "limbo" (Schwartz & Weintraub, 1974).

Needless to say, mothers whose spouses have suddenly been arrested and incarcerated are very preoccupied with numerous financial considerations, practical arrangements and their own emotional reactions to the recent event. They are embarrassed to think that neighbors are aware of their plight; they are both angry at the accused and at the same time, lonely in his absence. Morris (1967) notes that both the inmate in jail and his spouse, in the midst of their own adjustments, often share the view that children are "too young" to be affected by the father's imprisonment. Although they admit that their children had been giving them problems since the father's incarceration, mothers most often view behavorial problems or changes in sleeping patterns, etc., as a "nuisance" for them rather than as a symptom of the child's own confusion and turmoil.

Sentencing Day

Sentencing day confirms the reality of on-going incarceration for the first time. Prior to sentencing, most family members hope for the best and often disregard the fact that long-term imprisonment is likely even when the crime committed is severe (Fishman & Alissi, 1979). Reactions in court by family members are, more often than not, shock and disbelief. The immensity of their problems suddenly become overwhelming and many wives, mothers, etc., helplessly look for answers to the scores of questions they now must ask: "What does the sentence mean? When can I visit? Will he be hurt? How will I make it alone?" As a woman grapples with her important and bewildering concerns, the court proceeds to the next case and she is usually left entirely alone.

Initial Incarceration

Adjustment to the reality of incarceration after sentencing involves many problems and issues for family members. The emotional stress has been compared to the mourning experiences of individuals who have lost a loved one to death (Schwartz & Weintraub, 1974; Sack et al., 1976). Unlike death, however, imprisonment carries with it a social stigma. Because the offender has committed an act that is socially unacceptable, his family members are often thought of as criminals, too (Bakker et al., 1978; Schneller, 1975), and are denied normal social outlets for grieving. Instead of receiving loving support from close friends and relatives, they are often confronted with blame for the inmates' actions and suggestions to "leave the bum" before it is too late (Schwartz & Weintraub, 1974).

In addition to coping with social ostracism, a change in financial status and a range of conflicting emotions, women must also assume new roles as single parents and single heads of the household. One of their first tasks is to provide an explanation of the father's absence to his children. In many cases, mothers choose to deceive their children by claiming that the father is "at school," "in the army," "at sea," etc. (Morris, 1967; Wilner, Marks & Pogue, 1966). Pauline Morris (1967) noted in a study of over 400 families in England, that in 40% of the cases, the children did not know the whereabouts of their fathers.

Many reasons have been given as an explanation for the parents' deception. Mothers who withhold the truth about "daddy" often do so to preserve the father's image as a "good" person. Fathers, themselves, often fear that the truth will cause children to reject them or hate them and so instruct their spouses to avoid the issue (Morris, 1967). Some mothers feel that if they withhold the information, they may be able to protect the child from teasing by neighbors and classmates. In reality, children often sense the truth even when they have been told otherwise and see the mother's false explanation as a sign of personal rejection. Forced to accept the mother's duplicity, these children have no outlets for expressing their own grief and frustration.

A child's reaction to a father's incarceration can have many forms of expression. Most children appear preoccupied with their loss and are especially sad. Sack (1977), in interviews with 6 families of offenders noted that all of the children involved expressed a strong desire to have their fathers home and would sometimes blame their mothers for permitting the separation. The powerlessness of the mother to change the situation is a further threat to the child's already shaken sense of security (Sack, 1977).

As a result of the incarceration, its explanation and its effect on home life, children of offenders commonly display aggressive and antisocial behavior in an attempt to identify with the "lost" father in prison (Sack et al., 1976), suffer from feelings of guilt (Wilmer et al., 1966), and often fail to maintain previous performance levels in school (Friedman & Esselstyn, 1965). Some children experience eating problems, insomnia and clinging (Morris, 1967), a rupture in personal relationships with peers, and a loss in self-esteem (Sack et al., 1976). Although she notes that the severity of reactions to incarceration vary dramatically among children affected, Morris (1967) concludes that few children will escape the experience undamaged.

One of the few ways for families to maintain contact with the offender is through visiting. Authors who have written on the subject and practitioners who work with families of offenders agree that visiting is especially helpful for children because it calms their fears about their father's health and welfare as well as their concerns about his feelings for them (Weintraub, 1976; Sack, 1977; Wilmer et al., 1966). Children often have a predetermined image of prison from television or movies and can be very frightened or, conversely, impressed, before they actually see the institution.

Unfortunately, even though the first experience can calm a child's initial fears, ongoing visiting conditions are not conducive to emotionally satisfying visits and do not promote regular visiting patterns (Fishman & Cassin, 1981). Most institutions have very limited visiting hours and are located in remote areas which are cut off from major urban populations. As a result, transportation to the institution and scheduling can be overwhelming problems for the families involved (Schafer, 1977). Mothers with young children are often reluctant to undertake what will amount to an exhausting and expensive effort on a regular basis for a very limited amount of visiting.

Conditions in the visiting room itself also tend to inhibit visits. Inmates and their visitors are generally separated by barriers. In many institutions the barriers prohibit any touching whatsoever. Visits are usually under the close supervision of guards. The visiting room must accommodate the entire prison population and is usually crowded and noisy. There is generally a lack of privacy as well as a strict time limit to the visit, which can place a great deal of pressure on the family. Prison visiting rooms are usually drab and colorless. There is nothing to look at and, particularly for children, nothing to hold their interest while their parents converse. Usually a father is not permitted to hold his child. As a result, guards are often forced to admonish a man when his youngster eagerly reaches for him. If the child grows restless and disturbs others, mothers can be asked to remove them from the visiting room for the duration of the visit. Unless she has someone with her to watch the child, she must leave too. It is easy to understand how parents could become extremely frustrated under these conditions, and, for the sake of their own comfort and relationship, decide not to include the children during visits. Such a result for the children involved can mean that they experience greater feelings of loneliness for their father in prison.

Pre/Post Release

The period of time immediately preceding and following the inmate's release is especially traumatic for the offender and his family. Since the woman has usually become independent in his absence, she is reluctant to give up new responsibilities and return to her former role in the household (Fishman & Cassin, 1981). The inmate, on the other hand, visualizes his return home as a resumption of what life was like before his incarceration. Unrealistic expectations are often not resolved in brief conversations on visiting days and can lead to conflict upon the inmate's release. The particular needs of children at this time can be overlooked as the family struggles to redefine itself.

IMPACT OF INCARCERATION ON CHILDREN/FAMILIES OF FEMALE OFFENDERS

Arrest/Pre-Trial

Children whose mothers are incarcerated can experience further problems not facing children of male offenders in addition to those already described. When a man is arrested and sent to prison, he usually can rely on the wife to continue in the care of his child without a total disruption in the child's environment. However, since a great many women offenders are single parents, they must find alternate living arrangements for any children left behind. In many cases, women will not inform arresting officers that they have children because they fear that the children will be taken and placed in foster homes before they have had a chance to deal with the situation themselves (Dubose, 1977). Some children, therefore, come home to empty houses and are alone for hours or even overnight before someone assumes custody (Carroll, 1980). This situation causes anxiety and fear for both the mother, who is concerned about the children's welfare, and the children who do not know the reason for the parent's absence (Fishman & Cassin, 1981).

Eventually, most children are cared for by close relatives, usually a grandmother. Although only a minority of children are placed in foster homes, it is not uncommon for siblings to be separated in different homes for the entire period of incarceration (Dubose, 1977). Both the disruption in his physical environment and separation from his siblings contribute to a child's emotional turmoil already instigated by the loss of his mother.

Incarceration

Children of female offenders have a more difficult time maintaining contact with their mothers for several reasons:

1. Since women comprise such a small percentage of state and federal inmate populations, there are fewer correctional institutions for women. The institutions which do exist are usually located at a greater distance from the inmates' homes. Some states such as New Hampshire send their female offenders to facilities in neighboring states. Federal offenders are held in only five institutions scattered throughout the country (Carroll, 1980; Fishman & Cassin, 1981). Since travel to institutions housing women involves greater cost and additional time, frequent visits are often impossible. In a 1964 study of female offenders in California, Zalba (1964) found that almost half of the children in the study had not seen their mothers in prison.

2. Children must rely on their caretakers' willingness to bring them to the institution. In some instances, relatives or friends caring for the children have their own opinions about the inmate and are hesitant to sanction her behavior by bringing the children to visit. Children, in this situation, are torn between the need to see their mother and the need to receive the approval of the caretaker (Fishman & Cassin, 1981)

3. Visiting conditions within the institution are similar to those described for male prisons and tend to discourage visiting for the same reasons.

Pre/Post Release

Mothers returning to the community from prison cannot assume that they will easily resume custody of their children. Some women find that relatives are ultimately unwilling to relinquish care of the children (Carroll, 1980); others find it necessary to establish themselves by finding permanent housing and jobs before they want to undertake parental responsibilities. In a sample of women offenders, McGowan (1978) noted that 60% of first time offenders were expecting to regain custody of their children, while only 20% of repeat offenders shared that goal. McGowan further claims that one out of twelve children will undergo a permanent change in his/her living status as a result of the mother's incarceration. In a very few cases, that change is caused by the intervention of the state in terminating parental rights.

New York and Oregon recognize incarceration as grounds for removing the children without the parents' consent. Arizona and California can withhold parental rights if the parent is judged unfit as a result of her incarceration (Carroll, 1980).

INNOVATIVE PROGRAM FOR CHILDREN OF OFFENDERS

Although projects specifically designed to assist children of offenders are few and far between, several successful models do exist within the United States. One of the more effective programs is described below.

Sesame Street

Sesame Street projects in prison are highly publicized because of their creative concept and link with Children's Television Workshop (CTW), originators of the popular Sesame Street and Electric Company television programs. In 1974, officials at the Federal Correctional Institution in Fort Worth, Texas, consulted with CTW in the development of an experimental project designed to provide educational and entertaining activities for children on visiting days. In an effort to (1) alleviate congestion in the visiting room, (2) give parents the opportunity to communicate without the constant interruptions of young children, and (3) provide the children with an accepting environment in which to express their feelings about the prison, Fort Worth opened a special playroom adjacent to the visiting room itself. A group of inmates were selected as caregivers and trained to develop activities and programs based on Sesame Street curriculum. Participating children visited with their own relatives and entered the playroom when they became restless. In addition to providing a positive visiting experience for children and parents, the playroom enabled inmate participants to interact with youngsters in a new way and, thereby, be more effective parents themselves. The Sesame Street concept quickly spread to other minimum security federal institutions throughout the country. During 1979, in Connecticut, Women in Crisis adopted the model at Somers Correctional Institution and established the first Sesame Street playroom in a maximum security facility. After two years, parents are indicating that children are eager to visit the institution and often talk about their inmate friends at home; inmates and their families find visiting more rewarding; and correctional administrators have accepted the project as an important service to the institution. One inmate at Somers summarized the impact of the project on children when he said:

> They walk through the door, fearful and not sure what to expect. Even though they don't understand the concept, they know that prison is no good. Their fathers are in prison—that's kind of an emotional thing. They don't worry as much about that after meeting other inmates. They think if these guys are all right, their dads are okay too!

Support for Families

Although projects assisting families of offenders may not focus specifically on the problems of children, any help which attempts to alleviate turmoil within the family will ultimately affect the children as well. During the last decade, numerous programs for families of offenders have been created in communities across the country as more and more people recognize the tremendous need in this area. During the fall of 1981 the National Institute of Corrections awarded a grant to Women in Crisis to develop the first national document ever published which compiles (1) a thorough review of the literature on the subject, and (2) a complete listing of programs across the country that provide assistance to individuals with loved ones in prison.[1]

CONCLUSION

The special problems of children and other family members of offenders are far reaching and serious in their scope. Although there is still a tremendous need for increased services to alleviate the trauma of separation from incarceration, it is encouraging to see that the needs of families of offenders are finally being acknowledged as important on a widespread basis. Since families of offenders serve as sources of assistance to offenders and ex-offenders, the recognition and resolution of their concerns is a milestone in the field of criminal justice as well as an advance in the area of human service in general.

REFERENCE NOTE

1. For a copy of this document including the extensive bibliography, please write to the National Institute of Corrections, 320 First Street, N.W., Washington, D.C. 20534, and ask for *Services for Families of Offenders: An Overview*, by Susan Hoffman Fishman & Candace Cassin.

REFERENCES

Adams, D., & Fischer, J. The effects of prison residents' community contacts on recidivism rates. *Corrective and Social Psychiatry and Journal of Behavioral Technology, Methods and Therapy,* 1976, *22,* 21–27.

Bakker, L., Morris, B. A., & Janus, L. M. Hidden victims of crime. *Social Work,* 1978, *23,* 143–148.

Bureau of Justice Statistics. *Prisoners in state and federal institutions on December 31, 1978, national prisoner services bulletin.* Washington, D.C.: Law Enforcement Assistance Administration, National Criminal Justice Statistics Service, Department of Justice, 1979.

Carrol, H. Children of prisoners: Effects of parental absence. Yale University Child Study Center, 1980. Unpublished document.

Cobean, S. C., & Power, P. W. The role of the family in the rehabilitation of the offender. *International Journal of Offender Therapy and Comparative Criminology,* 1978, *22,* 29–39.

Dubose, P. Women in prison: A neglected issue. *Incarceration Benefits & Drawbacks.* University of Texas at Arlington, 1977.

Fishman, S. H. Losing a loved one to incarceration: The effect of imprisonment on family members. *The Personnel and Guidance Journal,* 1981, *59,* 372–375.

Fishman, S. H., & Alissi, A. S. Strengthening families as natural support systems for offenders. *Federal Probation,* 1979, *43,* 16–21.

Fishman, S. H., & Cassin, C. J. M. Services for families of offenders, an overview. *National Institute of Corrections, U.S. Department of Justice,* 1981.

Friedman, S., & Esselstyn, T. C. The adjustment of children of jail inmates. *Federal Probation,* 1965, *29,* 55–59.

Holt, N., & Miller, D. *Explorations in inmate-family relationships.* Sacramento, California: Research Division, Department of Corrections, 1972.

Homer, E. L. Inmate-family ties: Desirable but difficult. *Federal Probation,* 1979, *43,* 47–52.

LaPointe, V. Mothers inside, children outside: Some issues surrounding imprisoned mothers and their children. *Proceedings of the 107th Annual Congress of Corrections of the American Correctional Association,* 1977.

McGowan, B. G. Why punish the children? A study of children of women prisoners. *National Council on Crime & Delinquency,* 1978.

Morris, P. Fathers in prison. *British Journal of Criminology,* 1967, *7,* 424–430.

Morris, P. *Prisoners and their families.* New York: Holt Publishing Company, 1965.

Sack, W. H. Children of imprisoned fathers. *Psychiatry,* 1977, *40,* 163–174.

Sack, W., Seidler, J., & Thomas, S. The children of imprisoned parents: A psychological exploration. *American Journal of Orthopsychiatry,* 1976, *46,* 618–628.

Schafer, N. E. Prison visiting: A background for change. *Federal Probation,* 1978, *42,* 47–50.

Schneller, D. P. Some social and psychological effects of incarceration on the families of negro prisoners. *American Journal of Correction,* 1975, *37,* 29–33.

Schwartz, M., & Weintraub, J. The prisoner's wife: A study in crisis. *Federal Probation,* 1974, *38,* 20–26.

Weintraub, J. The delivery of services to families of prisoners. *Federal Probation,* 1976, *40,* 28–31.

Wilmer, H. A., Marks, I., & Pogue, E. Group treatment of prisoners and their families. *Mental Hygiene,* 1966, *50,* 380–389.

Zalba, S. R. *Women Prisoners and their Families.* Los Angeles: California Department of Corrections, 1964.